The USES of ABUNDANCE

A History of New Jersey's Economy

by PAUL G. E. CLEMENS

TRENTON
NEW JERSEY HISTORICAL COMMISSION, DEPARTMENT OF STATE

Printed in the United States of America

Reprint, 2001, Trenton Printing

New Jersey Historical Commission, Department of State
225 West State Street, P.O. Box 305
Trenton, New Jersey 08625

Designed by Nancy H. Dallaire and Lee R. Parks
Cover designed by Nancy H. Dallaire

Library of Congress Cataloging-in-Publication Data

Clemens, Paul G. E., 1947-
The uses of abundance: a history of New Jersey's economy by Paul G. E. Clemens.
p. cm.—(New Jersey history series; 2)
Includes bibliographical references.
ISBN 0-89743-078-6: $9.00
1. New Jersey—Economic conditions. 2. New Jersey—History. I. Title. II. Series.
HC107.N5C58 1992
330.9749—dc20 92-38149
CIP

TABLE OF CONTENTS

for

Sarah-Elizabeth
Jesse
Emilie

and all the others fortunate enough
to be educated in New Jersey

INTRODUCTION

Jacob Crammer was a farmer in Burlington County, New Jersey. When he died in 1766, he left little behind—a family, a will, and a small estate. After his death, New Jersey court officials ordered an appraisal of his estate to guard the interests of his heirs and creditors. As Jacob Crammer was not famous, the appraisal of his estate can tell us much about how ordinary people lived in colonial New Jersey. The appraisers' list is reproduced on page 8, along with their evaluation of each item in pounds (£), shillings (s), and pence (d)—the monetary units of the English-speaking world in the eighteenth century.*

Jacob Crammer's inventory, if carefully read, can tell us much about economic life in colonial New Jersey. Crammer's interest in farming is obvious, as he owned livestock and farm equipment; but he was something more than a farmer, for the appraisers noted as well carpenter's tools, a fishing boat, and a seine or fishing net. The money, bills owed, and debts on his books suggest Crammer was not entirely self-sufficient, but rather bought and bartered some of what he needed from his neighbors. Signs of comfortable living were few. Beds, some furniture, and wearing apparel, worth about one-fifth of the entire estate value, were Crammer's only amenities—all he had that indicated he did anything but farm, fish, and work at a craft. Either Jacob Crammer was very poor and had no money to purchase household luxuries, or he invested whatever profits he made in the farm itself in the hope of making it more productive.

*There were twenty shillings in a pound and twelve pence in a shilling. Monetary amounts were written " £14 19s. d.," " £14.19.6," or "14/19/6."

An Inventory of the Goods of Jacob Crammer taken on the 21st Day of July 1766[1]

	£	s	d
Money and wearing apparel	5	08	00
Beds, furniture, and household goods	15	18	00
Stock of cattle	31	10	00
Sheep	3	00	00
One hog		10	00
Two horses and a saddle	9	05	00
Hides and skins		10	00
Eight hives of bees	2	00	00
Fishing boat, canoe, part of a seine	4	00	00
Gun and powder horn		12	00
Farmer's and carpenter's tools	9	19	00
Bills owed and debts on his books	24	17	00
Total	107	09	00

As informative as the appraisal of Jacob Crammer's estate is, then, the document raises as many questions as it answers. How complete a picture of Crammer's economic activities does the record provide? Did he have no land? No farm buildings? No crops? And even if the appraisal is complete, how typical was Crammer of the people of New Jersey? Were most other people farmers? Were they richer or poorer than he was? Did Crammer's accomplishments represent an improvement on the position of earlier generations of colonists? Did he contribute to the development of New Jersey or in some way damage the environment and burden future generations?

These questions, as they relate to all the people of New Jersey, not just Jacob Crammer, comprise the heart of this pamphlet. First comes the problem of growth and welfare. When and why did economic growth begin in New Jersey? Who gained, who lost (for example, how were wealth and income redistributed) as a consequence of growth? Second, what was

NOTE: Spelling and punctuation have been modernized in all quotations and tables throughout this book.

the structure of New Jersey's economy? What mix was there of occupations in the colonial period, and how did that structure change? How creatively did individuals respond to new market opportunities? Third, what was the cost of progress? What can be said about the way the developing economic system has affected the quality of life in New Jersey?

If we return briefly to Jacob Crammer and assume that he was typical, then we can clarify these themes. Growth: When Crammer died in 1766 he owned £107 in property. Was this more than people owned earlier, say in 1700? Welfare: Were most people in 1766 about as wealthy as Crammer, or were many poorer or more prosperous than he? Structure: Crammer was a farmer. How many farmers lived in New Jersey in 1766 compared to merchants, blacksmiths, laborers, and others? Cost: Did Crammer ruin the soil by farming it too intensively? Did he help the economy by introducing new breeds of sheep or cattle?

These questions will focus this pamphlet on two fundamental transitions. The first is New Jersey's transition from an agricultural economy (Chapter One) to an industrial economy (Chapter Two); the second is the shift from a producer society (also Chapter Two) to a consumer society (Chapter Three). If one purpose of this work is to explain these fundamental changes, the other is to understand the economic history of the state in human terms, as laborers, industrialists, and farmers such as Jacob Crammer lived it.

The author wishes to thank Kathleen V. Jones, Emilie Jones, Stanley Worton, Barbara Petrick and Mary R. Murrin for help with this essay.

CHAPTER ONE

The Agricultural Economy of Early New Jersey, 1600–1800

The Lenape Indians and the First Economy

Well before Europeans came in the early seventeenth century to lands the English would name East and West Jersey, the Lenape—or Original People—were here. What struck the early Dutch and English colonists was how different—in language, religion, skin color, and way of life—the Lenape were from themselves. They spoke Algonquian, not Dutch or English. They worshiped neither the wrathful God of the English and Dutch Calvinists nor the more peaceful and personal God of the English Quakers, but a force or spirit present everywhere. The Lenape (whites would call them the Delaware Indians) moved their villages occasionally rather than settle permanently in one place. If the European colonists ignored many similarities between themselves and the Native Americans, they nonetheless were certainly aware that they shared one thing with them. All were agricultural peoples.

The economic history of New Jersey begins with the Lenape. They lived by farming in small villages, which they left to hunt and fish only when they had accomplished the primary tasks of planting, cultivating and harvesting food crops. When repeated use had worn the soil and decreased its fertility, the Lenape shifted to new land, and, if necessary, to new village sites. But basically they were a sedentary people, attached to their villages and preoccupied with the demands of growing food.

The Lenape raised maize, which Europeans knew as corn. "At the end of March," Isaack De Rasieres, a Dutch settler, observed in 1628, "they begin to break up the earth with mattocks, which they buy from us for the skins of beavers and otters." (Before contact with the Europeans, the Lenape had fashioned agricultural tools from bones and wood.) They then formed the earth into mounds two and a half feet from each other, and in April sowed a half-dozen seeds in each mound. "In the middle of May," De Rasieres continued, "when the maize is the height of a finger or more, they plant in each heap three or four Turkish beans [probably kidney beans], which they grow up with and against the maize, which serves for props."[1] Then followed two difficult months of weeding and cultivation, the thinning-out of poor ears in August, and finally the picking.

But that was only half the work. To convert ears of maize to bread or porridge, the Lenape, De Rasieres wrote, "first boil it and then beat it flat upon a stone; then they put it into a wooden mortar, which they know how to hollow out by fire, and then they have a stone pestle .... with which they pound it small, and sift it through a small basket" that they had woven from rushes.[2] The meal could then be kneaded into dough or boiled into a porridge. In addition to maize and beans, the Lenape also grew squash, pumpkins, and sunflowers as food crops.

Since the summers called for intense field labor, the Lenape hunted, fished and gathered during the other seasons. David de Vries, who wrote of his stay from 1636 to 1644 in New Netherland (the Dutch name for New York) and Ackingh-sack (the Dutch settlement in the Hackensack Valley), spoke of deer, bear, elk, wolves, wildcats, beaver, mink, and otter in the Delawares' hunting grounds. He described a hunt where a hundred or more men stood in a line many paces from each other and "holding flat thigh-bones in the hand, beat [the bones] with a stick, and so drive the creatures before them to the river. As they approach the river, they close nearer to each other, and whatever is between any two of them, is at the mercy of their bows and arrows, or must take to the river."[3]

In the river, the Delawares would lasso and drown the deer. More commonly, hunters formed a large circle around a game area, uprooted enough grass to prevent fire from spreading in the wrong direction, and then ignited the brush and followed the flames as they drove the trapped animals toward an ever-smaller area at the center of the circle. With equal skill, the Lenape systematically caught large quantities of fresh and saltwater fish, or, in a more leisurely fashion, gathered chestnuts, grapes, sweet berries, and wild rice.

Women and men performed different but related agricultural tasks. Men cleared the fields of trees and broke the soil, but here their work ended, as the 1628 account of De Rasieres makes clear: "It is grain to which much labor is given, with weeding and earthing-up, or it does not thrive, and to this the women must attend very closely. The men would not once look to it, for it would compromise their dignity too much."[4] While women did the fieldwork (among the English and Dutch, in contrast, men generally planted and tended crops), the men and boys would hunt in the nearby woods or fish in the local rivers, thus helping to maintain the village food supply. Women, generally with their children, tended gardens, searched the woods for nuts and berries, and worked wild hemp into strands for fishing nets. In the summer, families near the coast could take canoes to the sea, fish and gather oysters. After the fall harvest, whole villages, the old people excepted, embarked on hunting trips.

After the coming of whites, the Lenape population declined steadily. A recent estimate has put the precontact population at between twenty-four hundred and six thousand; in 1684, about half a century after Dutch and English settlers arrived in East Jersey, the deputy governor of the colony reported that there were few "Indian Natives" remaining. By the middle of the eighteenth century, there were no more than three hundred left in New Jersey.

The precipitous decline of the Lenape population had three causes. Warfare took many lives. Distrust and misunderstanding on both sides led to arguments, murders, and brutal retaliatory raids. Europeans, believing themselves superior, were all too ready to simply eliminate the Lenape. Of equal significance in the decline of the Lenape was their loss of land. They sold some of it outright and by mutual consent, bargained some away without a clear notion of what was being given up, and lost some through fraud, until the land they needed for planting and hunting had passed from them to the Dutch and English. After this, the Lenape left to seek new homes in the country's interior. Yet it was a third factor, disease, that may well have struck the hardest blow at the Lenape. Europeans brought with them diseases—primarily respiratory ailments and smallpox—against which Native Americans had no immunities, and which killed much of the Native American population throughout the New World.

In sum, what can be said of the first people and first economy of New Jersey? The Lenapes' goal was self-sufficiency; farming, hunting, fishing, and gathering all helped them achieve this. Their success resulted from a balance between population and food supply; they lived as well as they did because each band of Lenape had a large geographical area with abundant animal and plant resources and sufficient fertile land. In contrast to the Dutch and English, who came from nations where market exchange for profit already governed much of agricultural life, the Lenape had little desire to accumulate wealth or goods. They farmed communally without specializing in particular tasks as Europeans did. And before contact with Europeans, they obtained most of what they needed directly through their own labor rather than through trade with other communities or distant peoples. Theirs was a life that was simpler yet in most ways as plentiful as that of seventeenth-century Europeans. English and Dutch settlement forever ended the Lenape way of life in New Jersey.

Settlement and Population Growth to 1800

Unlike most North American colonies, New Jersey was not settled by a single group of Europeans; rather, several distinct peoples, from three nations, arrived between the 1630s and 1670s. The Dutch arrived first, crossing the Hudson in 1629 from their trading outpost at New Amsterdam (Manhattan), to a site which today is Jersey City. For three decades conflict with the Lenape restricted Dutch movement into the Hackensack Valley, but by 1660 they had prevailed, erected a garrison town at Bergen, and established substantial farmsteads west of the Hudson River (see the map).

Swedish traders established Fort Nya Elfsborg (near Salem) on the lower Delaware River in 1643, moving north from the outpost of the New Sweden Company at Fort Christina (near

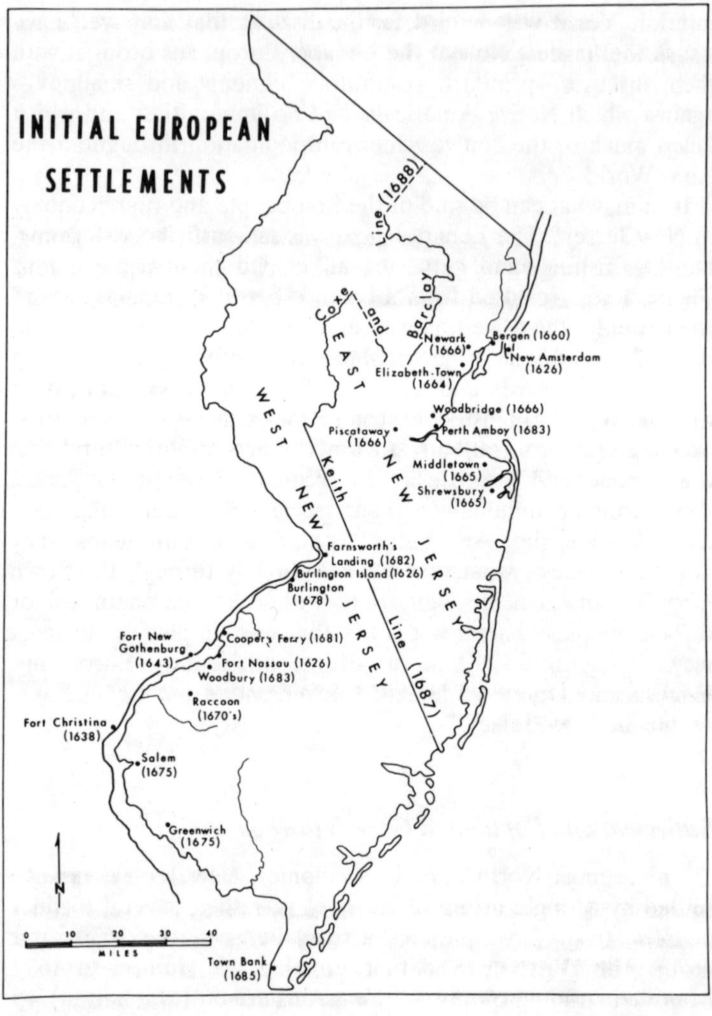

Initial European settlements in New Jersey. *From Peter O. Wacker,* Land & People: A Cultural Geography of Preindustrial New Jersey: Origins and Settlement Patterns *(New Brunswick, 1975), p. 122. Reprinted by permission of* RUTGERS UNIVERSITY PRESS.

Wilmington, Delaware). Swedes played a critical role in the tangled European relations with the Lenape, but few established farms or settled permanently. At the close of the colonial period no more than 10 percent of the population of southern New Jersey was of Swedish extraction.

English involvement began in the 1660s. In 1664, Charles II, king of England, granted the New York–New Jersey region to his brother James, duke of York. Of course, the Dutch already occupied the Hudson River Valley. James dealt with this inconvenience by sending a fleet to New Amsterdam and forcing the surrender of the Dutch government. Needing people for the colony, the English let the Dutch settlers remain. Meanwhile, James conveyed his grant of New Jersey to two supporters, Sir George Carteret and John, Lord Berkeley. After a decade of complicated maneuvers, the Carteret claim became the basis for the establishment of East Jersey and the Berkeley claim for West Jersey, a division agreed to in 1676.

Settlers did not wait for English politicians to decide who owned what. The first English people to jump at the opportunity New Jersey offered were New Englanders. Puritans (formerly members of Congregationalist churches in Connecticut) laid out Elizabeth-Town in 1664, and Newark and Woodbridge in 1666. New England Baptists settled Middletown and Piscataway, and Quakers founded Shrewsbury. The towns were powerful magnets, and by 1680 over three thousand English settlers had flocked to them.

A few years later the English began moving just as rapidly into West Jersey. John Fenwick led fellow members of the Society of Friends (Quakers) to Salem, and within the next decade Quakers pushed up the Delaware, establishing towns as they went. In 1676, George Carteret officially deeded West Jersey over to Quaker proprietors (that is, people to whom the king of England granted ownership of the land and the right to establish government in West Jersey). One of these was William Penn, who purchased a proprietary interest in West Jersey and established a Quaker colony in Pennsylvania. His vigorous efforts to persuade fellow English people to settle along the Delaware brought new women and men to the region. A number of Scots also became West Jersey proprietors, and emigration from Scotland followed. By the end of the century, some three thousand settlers lived in West Jersey.

What explains the initial settlement of East and West Jersey? In 1681 an anonymous pamphlet writer, working on behalf of the West Jersey proprietors, spelled out some of the attractions. First, passage was relatively cheap: "The Price for every Passenger, (that is to say) for Men and Women, Meat, Drink, and Passage, with a Chest, is Five Pounds sterling per Head [a little more than the cost of a horse]: For Children of Twelve Years of Age, and under, Fifty Shillings [the cost of a cow]; Suckling Children, Nothing." Next, there was self-government: "Neither Customs, Charge, Imposition, nor any other Services or Taxes whatsoever, are to be Imposed upon the Inhabitants, but by their own Consent in a Free and General-Assembly." Third, there was the promise of toleration: "There is . . . Provision made for Liberty of Conscience, in Matters of Religion, that all Persons living Peaceably, may injoy the Benefit of Religious Exercise thereof, without any Molestation whatever." And finally, there was a dual expectation that the soil was good and "capable to produce any thing that England doth . . . far Greater" and that land itself was abundant and inexpensive.[5]

While each of these factors attracted particular immigrants, a more general explanation can be offered for the large number of settlers. Between the 1620s and 1680s, England's population grew rapidly, its cost of living rose, and employment opportunities diminished. An ever-larger, young, restless, and underemployed population saw an opportunity for something better in the colonies. Such immigrants were generally under twenty-five and often in their teens, more often male than female, generally unmarried, and usually too poor to pay their own passage to the New World. They came as servants with contracts to work for a given number of years in return for free passage. They were joined by free, better-off immigrants, who usually traveled with families and who were escaping religious and political troubles in England as well as looking for new opportunities in a new world.

English colonization began in Virginia, the West Indies, and Massachusetts; few English people went to New Jersey at first. But as the flow of immigrants continued and the best farming land in the original settlements was taken, colonizing efforts shifted to new areas. In the 1660s and 1670s the Delaware and

Hudson valleys, and the Carolinas to the south, became the focus for the continuing migration of Old World people to North America.

After 1680, population growth depended as much on natural increase (the excess of births over deaths) as on immigration. In 1680, the population of New Jersey was probably a little over 4,000; by 1726, the date of the first reliable census, it had increased to about 30,000. In 1745, there were 61,300 residents in New Jersey; by 1784, after the conclusion of the American Revolution, some 150,000 people lived in the state, and when the new century began, federal census takers counted 211,000.

New Jersey's black and white populations grew together. For the seventeenth century, there is ample evidence that the Dutch and English used slaves in East Jersey, but the first reliable colony-wide count of the black population came with the 1726 census. In that year there were 2,581 blacks in New Jersey, constituting about eight percent of the population. The proportion of blacks in the population remained fairly constant through 1800, when there were 12,400 slaves and 4,400 free blacks.

Thus a remarkable mix of peoples—English, Dutch, Africans, Scots, Scots-Irish (Scots who had resettled in northern Ireland before leaving for America), Irish, and Germans—made New Jersey as ethnically and religiously diverse a colony as any in North America. Because of the healthy climate and bountiful resources, each new settler group continued to grow in number even as immigration slowed.

Agricultural Economy

Most of New Jersey's rapidly growing free population lived by farming, and, according to early reports, they lived well. Gabriel Thomas pictured the Burlington area in 1698 as follows: the market town had "many fine stately Brick-Houses built, and a commodious Dock for Vessels to come in at .... Likewise in the said Town there are very many fine Wharfs and large Timber-Yards, Malt-Houses, Brew Houses, Bake Houses; and most sorts of Trades-Men .... As for Corn, they have Wheat, Rye, Pease, Oates, Barley, Rice, etc., in vast quantities: Also Indian-Corn, Pease and Beans, likewise English Hemp and Flax, which prospers [in West Jersey] exceedingly."[6] Thomas went on to boast of the wild food, game animals, fertile soil, and assortment of fish as if the Delaware River valley were a bountiful Garden of Eden.

In reality, of course, even such abundance did not make settlement easy. The Lenape had learned to live from the region's resources with a minimum of effort; their wants were few and different. They valued leisure more than the accumulation of wealth. Europeans came to take and tame the land. They would improve what they found: cut, clear, build, fence, plow and plant, drive off the predatory wildlife, and introduce domesticated livestock. Always busy, always working (church days excepted), Europeans reshaped New Jersey's economy.

Farming is hard work; for the initial settlers, it was even harder. Establishing a farmstead required several years of daily, backbreaking toil. Land had to be cleared of trees, the soil broken with plow and harrow, homes and barns erected, fences built to contain cattle and sheep. Nothing got done overnight. First homes were more often copies of Lenape dwellings than reproductions of the clapboard and brick designs familiar to Europeans. Swine ran wild in the woods for years before fencing became commonplace, and cattle died during the winter for lack of barns. Farmers burned fields clear rather than axe and uproot trees. The initial crops were basic—corn and vegetables (which the Lenape also grew) and wheat (the standard English grain). For most first-generation settlers the chief accomplishment was establishing a working homestead. A functioning farm represented a significant accumulation of capital and a tangible inheritance that assured the well-being of a family's sons and daughters.

What was farming life like for the established landowners of subsequent generations? Erkuries Beatty kept an unusually detailed diary of how he managed his farm near Princeton at the close of the eighteenth century. The daily entries listed below give some sense of the seasonal responsibilities of farm life.

Spring

April 6th: Returned from New Brunswick; carpenters at work; broke wagon; Isaac and Tom Robinson [hired laborers] finished plowing the near quarter; Isaac finished sowing timothy seed in orchard.

April 30th: Mr. Reid and Isaac [workers] invited for Wednesday [April 26th] and on that day we got [the barn] up very easy without any accident and the cow shed too . . . . We had 32 people at the raising and gave them all supper; at least twice as many people as we wanted, but I was happy I had so many friends.

Summer

July 6th: Isaac cut Virginia wheat today; very poor but a good deal of timothy which obliged us to let it lie in swath, but it will make fine fodder. In afternoon Ben harrowed down corn having only plowed one furrow around it, but it being very dry and no seeds or grass concluded it would do with plowing out middles. Mare foaled colt.

July 11th: My Stars.—a shower of rain last night has wet all my rye . . . . May help corn; Isaac finished cropping buckwheat ground in morning. Put rye in Dutch shack to dry and sun came out. Cut remaining rye.

Fall

September 27: Commencement [at Princeton] and a great many people of all sorts, sizes, descriptions, and colors.

October 15th: Walked over farm. Rye up poor. Frost killed everything. Time to dig potatoes and husk corn.

October 30th: We all husked corn until night and we was tired.

November 26th: On Saturday, Isaac hauled wood and put flax in hay house; prepare to kill hogs and beef on Monday.

Winter

December 22nd: Went to Trenton with 19½ bushels of poor wheat which only weigh about 17 bushels 3 peck when I got there; not clean; M. Milnor only allowed me but 10/6 a bushel for it. December 26th: Isaac breaking flax and me riding about paying some of my small debts.

January 6th: To New Brunswick with sled and barley; sold for 6/6 only. Returned with a few boards. Isaac hunting rabbits.[7]

Even this limited group of diary entries gives a revealing picture of early New Jersey's agricultural economy. Farming was diversified: no one crop (staple) predominated. Beatty mentioned rye, timothy, barley, wheat, corn, potatoes, and flax, as well as the livestock he raised to slaughter. He harvested at least part of his crop for the market and traveled considerable distances to sell wheat (Trenton) and barley (New Brunswick). He hired laborers to work year-round in his fields and carpenters to help with a farm structure, but when it came to putting up his barn, Beatty relied on friends and neighbors. If the work was hard, it was also varied: there were endless tasks to do, and mornings and afternoons were generally spent at different work. Spring planting gave way to summer and fall harvests and to a winter of hauling wood, hunting small game, and fixing things around the farm.

But there was more to farm life than Beatty's diary records. He was unmarried, and missing from his entries is any recognition of the contribution women made to the farm economy. For this we must turn to the diary of Elizabeth Crane, mother of ten children and wife of a farmer-carpenter, who lived in Hudson County in the Passaic Valley. The diary dates from the 1820s, but the routine of farm life was little different from that of the eighteenth century.

Spring (1824)
March 29th: Stuck out some currant bushes.
April 2nd: Sent 25 yards of kersey [linen] to Warner's to be woven.
May 11th: Weather very fine. Father, Vester [son], and Pete Hill washed the sheep. Went to John Marshall's. Raising his barn. Went to Vreeland's to get Mary's shoes mended. Mary [daughter] went to sow tow . . . Writing school commenced. Daniel [son] covered 15 rows of corn.

Summer
June 28th: Rainy for part of the day. I weighed 29 pounds of marino wool. Debby [daughter] made three pair of gloves. Mary spooled Aunt Deborah's piece. Father and Vester worked in the shop. Father paid Mulford Day one dollar. Daniel plowed corn. Black Bill [free black hired worker] drawing dung. Harriet and Elizabeth [daughter] got canvas to make them samplers.

Fall
October 30th: Snow squall and cold, no frost until night before last to kill the blossoms. Meeting [Methodist] today; five persons dipped in the river at the mouth of Salt Brook. All

gone to Meeting tonight. Father and the boys making cider today.

November 25th: Clear and colder. Great firing in New York. Father and the boys drawing stalks. Myself making candles.

Winter

February 7th: Clear and warmer. Father and Vester getting wood. The girls have spun 50 pounds of flax this winter. The sleighing begins to be poor.[8]

These entries reflect a family at work, the father and sons in the fields or in the carpenter shop, the mother and daughters spinning, making candles, or in the orchard. Women produced cloth, bread, butter, cheese, and many other items essential to a family's welfare.

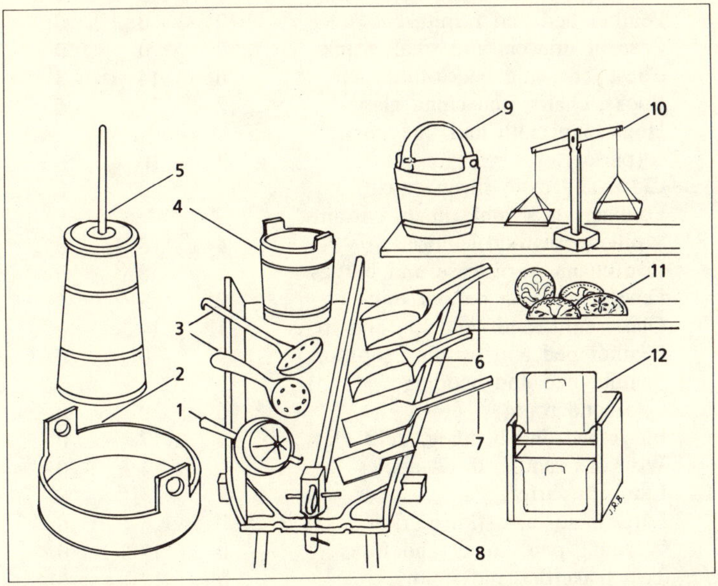

Butter-making tools. *(1) strainer, (2) keeler, (3) skimmers, (4) sour cream tub, (5) churn, (6) scoops, (7) butter workers, (8) working table, (9) firkin, (10) scale, (11) prints, (12) butter box. Reprinted from* Tools & Trades of America's Past: The Mercer Collection *(Doylestown, Pa., 1981), by permission of the* MERCER MUSEUM OF THE BUCKS COUNTY HISTORICAL SOCIETY.

Diaries such as those of Betsy Crane and Erkuries Beatty give a good sense of the daily routine on early New Jersey farms, but they tell us less about the rewards of farm labor. Did farm families simply try to get by year after year, or did people like Beatty and Crane want to improve their homesteads, accumulate possessions, and live more comfortably? A different type of document, a probate inventory or appraisement, provides some sense of how well farm families did. This one is for the estate of Hudson Middleton, a yeoman (landed farmer) from Chester, Burlington County, who died in 1767.

Inventory of the Goods of Hudson Middleton taken on the 18th and 19th of January 1768.[9]

	£	s	d
Wearing apparel (lodging room)	12	15	4
Feather bed and furniture	12	0	0
Case of drawers and small trunk	2	0	0
Chest, box, and bedclothes	8	14	3
Books, chairs, and china glass	2	11	6
Homespun cloth and fine linen (parlor)	3	10	6
Clock and case, silver watch	11	0	0
Looking glass, table linen, curtains, pillowcases and sundries	4	8	0
Five chairs, yarn, case and bottles	2	8	0
Pewter and iron pepper mill	2	15	6
Glass, delft, and sundries, end irons	1	14	0
Feather bed and bedding (upstairs)	9	0	0
Feather bed and bedding (second room)	6	0	0
Flock bed and bedding, delft glass	3	17	0
Woman's saddle, dried apples	1	4	0
Lumber (garret)	2	5	0
Large pine table (kitchen)	0	6	0
Warming pan, knives and forks	0	17	0
Two teakettles and sundries	0	17	6
Scales, weights, steelyards, spoons	1	4	6
Wheel, chairs, settle, dough trough	1	2	0
Candlesticks, bake irons, pot rack, end iron	1	11	0

Iron pots, skillets	2	18	0
Beef, wooden and earthenware, candles (milk room)	4	11	0
Still, worm, and tub (still house)	10	0	0
Grindstone and crank	0	5	0
Bridle and saddle, farm gears	2	13	0
Brass kettle, pails and sundries	0	14	3
Cider and empty casks (big cellar)	3	8	6
Earthenware, hogs lard (little cellar)	2	0	2
Pork and tubs for the same (little cellar)	11	0	0
Beds and bedding (kitchen chamber)	3	0	0
Bags and flower, wheels and sundries	2	16	0
Iron and lumber	2	17	0
Bond and note interest	83	16	10
Negro boy named Sipeo	50	0	0
Negro boy named Sam	40	0	0
Negro boy named Job	15	0	0
24 sheep, 9 cows	45	5	0
Two heifers calf and bull	11	10	0
Yoke of oxen	10	10	0
Yoke of steers	9	10	0
Brown horse, black colt	17	10	0
Bay mare, bay colt	17	0	0
Brown horse	12	0	0
2 sows and 32 shoats	14	2	6
Five geese and dunghill fowl	1	6	3
Harrow and harrow plough	1	10	6
Ox cart and little wagon	9	0	0
80 bushels of indian corn	10	13	4
19 bushels of wheat	5	14	0
25 bushels of rye	4	17	6
3 bushels of oats	0	7	6
Hay in stacks and barns	11	15	0
Rakes, riddle, and sundries (barn)	0	10	0
12 bushels of buckwheat	1	10	0
Cider mill, press, trough, cheese press	1	17	6
Small hive of bees, harrow, hog trough	0	15	6
Chains, hogshead, tub	1	0	6
Pair of wagon parts	0	7	0
Green wheat and rye in the ground	16	6	0
Total	531	19	5

Middleton's inventory suggests a great deal about New Jersey farming in the Delaware River region. Like Beatty, he practiced diversified agriculture, not only harvesting grain crops but producing cheese from milk, milling cider from apples, and obtaining honey from beehives. His investments in tools were limited—a harrow and plow for field work, a cart to collect crops and haul wood, and a wagon for marketing. In his fields he kept a substantial number of sheep and cows. Nothing indicates whether he hired wage laborers or employed his children on the farm, but the inventory includes three slaves, Sipeo, Sam, and Job. In his will he freed a fourth. (As often happened, the three slaves mentioned in the inventory were separated at their owner's death, each going to a different heir.)

Middleton lived modestly. His house was clearly substantial: it had two floors and two cellars, a separate kitchen and parlor, and several bedrooms, so that it offered considerably more privacy than the one-room log cabins of the first generation. Beds abounded. He owned pewterware, Delft china, and crystal for the dinner table, numerous utensils and pepper for cooking, and a watch and clock, both luxuries as well as reminders that a prosperous farmer used time wisely. But one should also be struck by what is not in the inventory: there was very little furniture to fill such a large house—no bookcase, no desk, no corner cabinet, and only a pine table. If coffee and pewter were listed, tea and cinnamon were not; if Delft china was used, there were none of the specialized dishes—butter dishes, cream pots—that were becoming ever more common in eighteenth-century England.

Taken as a whole, in fact, Middleton's inventory indicates that he accumulated most of his wealth by investing time, energy, and profits in building up his farm. His most valuable assets were his cleared fields, his cattle, his home, and the three slave children. Beyond this, his surplus went primarily into loans (worth £ 83.16.10), with the only household items of any note being his beds and bedding. His success was not a result of sophisticated tools (recall how few he had) or well-fertilized soils. Except for cow and sheep dung, he probably didn't use fertilizer. It was the result of simple hard work, reinvestment in land, labor, and livestock, and, as with Erkuries Beatty, careful attention to the seasonal requirements of agricultural husbandry.

How typical was Hudson Middleton? Burlington County, because of its proximity to the Philadelphia market and its Quaker settlement, was among the wealthier regions of early New Jersey. Farms were large (averaging 150 acres) in comparison to the Dutch and English plots in East Jersey. As a landowner, Middleton was among the more securely established members of the community. Younger residents (at least half of all free adult males) more often lived in someone else's home and helped with agricultural labor or rented small tracts where they could combine gardening, growing a little grain and craft work. Middleton's landed neighbors, who made up the other half of the free population, were virtually all farmers, but among them were men with second occupations as tanners, millers, merchants or sawmill operators. In terms of wealth, an estate of £541 placed Middleton in the middle of the landowning class; his nonlanded neighbors, who were tenants and laborers, were unlikely to have a tenth of what he owned, while his landed friends as often as not had accumulated more than he.

In part, the prosperity of middling farmers such as Middleton, Beatty and Crane reflected the fact that their homesteads were relatively self-sufficient. Even small farms could produce much of what was necessary for life, and larger farms were virtually little plantation communities. William Kelly, to take another example, had an East Jersey estate in Morris County on which in 1768 he had

> a fine nursery of several thousand apple trees, ... a good farmhouse, kitchen, and a very fine dairy, and cider house built this year, a barn, with nine barracks for hay and corn; a very fine corn house, and a large granary; a Negro house, smokehouse, a large fowl house, a smith's shop, a coalhouse, a large cow house, two horse stables, two greenhouses to preserve cabbage and roots in the winter; a pigeon house, well stocked.[10]

Even for gentlemen farmers such as William Kelly, however, self-sufficiency was not so much a matter of producing everything they needed themselves as it was being part of an agricultural community with enough different occupations to supply most of the needs of a rural population. Thus most Jersey townships had gristmills for grinding flour, sawmills for cutting timber, and tanneries for making leather. At such shops and mills, farmers exchanged produce for services, just as they bartered farm goods with neighbors. Local exchange of goods (homespun linen), labor (so many days of plowing), and crops (corn), usually done without any use of money, kept rural households comfortably supplied with the necessities of life.

Yet there was more to the economy than this. Farmers prospered because it was a market economy: crops, land and labor were all commodities to be sold. Once a family had sufficient food for the winter, it hauled its surplus wheat, rye, beef and pork to the nearest market town. Land, as well, could be readily sold. In Europe, the rights of heirs and landlords often kept a family from selling the land they held; in New Jersey, land could be marketed and the hard work of improving property turned to monetary advantage.

Just as important, prosperous farmers could buy labor. For the payment of wages in cash or kind (that is, farm produce), householders could hire workers. Most laborers were young males and either recent immigrants or older local children. Other farmers bought the labor contracts of indentured servants and redemptioners (people who redeemed passage across the ocean with labor). Still others took on apprentices, young boys and girls who received room, board and training at a craft, in farming, or in housekeeping in return for yearly labor.

Slavery was probably as important as any of these labor arrangements. Africans, bound for life and forced to work, were (as we have noted) a remarkably large part of New Jersey's early population. While most slaves were agricultural laborers, many learned additional skills, and as this advertisement from the February 6, 1772, *Pennsylvania Journal* indicates, such skills often gave blacks an opportunity to escape enslavement.

> RUNAWAY from [James Miller] at Bladensburgh, in Maryland, a Negro man, EZEKIEL, born in the Jerseys, 30 years old, 5 feet 10 or 11 inches tall, thin-faced, slim-made, and very active, speaks good English and Low Dutch, is very plausible in his discourse, and crafty in his behavior .... He can make coarse shoes and for five years past worked at his former master's Starr Forge, on Stillwater, in Sussex County, New Jersey .... Whoever apprehends the said Negro ... shall receive FORTY SHILLINGS.[11]

Typically, of course, masters kept control of their slaves, and with such laborers they were able to clear and cultivate more land as market conditions warranted, and to reap the benefits of a thriving rural economy.

The grains and meat produced by free and servile labor on New Jersey farms entered the Atlantic commercial system. Local merchants, who usually shipped out of New York City or Philadelphia, sent wheat, corn, lumber, meat, cider, and dairy products to distant markets and imported manufactured goods, wine, rum, sugar, and molasses as well as slaves.

There were three principal markets for New Jersey produce: the West Indies, Southern Europe and New England. West Indian planters had converted much of the acreage on Barbados, Antigua, and Jamaica to sugar production. They had to import virtually all the corn and meat they needed to feed thousands of slave laborers. Supplying this demand stimulated commercial farming throughout the grain-growing colonies of North America, including New Jersey. Southern Europe (Spain and Portugal) was the second important market, and after the failure of Mediterranean wheat harvests in the mid-eighteenth century this region became even more important than the sugar islands as a market for grains. Mediterranean demand for food pushed up wheat prices from Virginia to Massachusetts and helped farmers such as Hudson Middleton afford the watches, Delft plates and other consumer goods that they wanted.

The New England market was less spectacular and more complicated. Blight destroyed New England's wheat-growing potential, so periodically food had to be imported for home consumption. Most other goods were imported by New Englanders simply to be reexported. Thus a Boston merchant bought New Jersey corn to send to the West Indies, covered the purchase by shipping to Perth Amboy manufactured goods which he had imported from England, and in exchange for the sale of the corn in Barbados acquired rum that he dispatched to Burlington. Complicated, but typical.

The only important nonfarm product shipped from New Jersey was iron. In many of the colony's isolated forests were forges and furnaces that produced iron for distant markets. Perhaps the most notable example was the Ringwood Furnace, operated in the Ramapo mountain region during the 1760s by

Peter Hasenclever, a German immigrant. Hasenclever bought the furnace after seeing an advertisement in the March 5, 1764, *New York Mercury:*

> To be sold, a new well-built furnace, good iron mines near the same, two forges, one with 3, and the other one with 2 fires; a sawmill, several dwelling-houses and coal houses, and several tracts of land adjoining; carts, wagons, utensils and tools proper for the works: the furnace and forges are situated on a good stream, 28 miles from Acquackanung landing, and 36 miles from Newark.[12]

Hasenclever revitalized Ringwood. He dammed Taxito Pond with an 860-foot-long, 22-foot-high dam, and then ran water by canal from the pond to waterwheels on the Ringwood River. He recruited skilled laborers from Germany, bought indentured servants, and during the Revolutionary War employed blacks and captive Hessian soldiers. Situated away from any established communities, Ringwood had to be turned into a self-sufficient plantation. Gristmills, sawmills, a store, school and church, and rented farm lands nearby all helped. Surrounding his plantation was the heavily timbered forest needed to make charcoal for the furnace, and overlooking the Ringwood Iron Manor (as it was then entitled) was Hasenclever's own impressive stone-and-lumber house.

Hasenclever got his ore with black powder from nearby mines, the standard practice in the East Jersey highlands. To the south, operations such as Charles Read's Batsto Furnace, upstream from Little Egg Harbor, used bog ore from deposits along swamps, wet meadows, and rivers. The virtually uninhabited expanses of the Pine Barrens provided fuel. Finished products—bar iron, pig iron, pots, kettles, and the like—could be readily carried to the Atlantic and sent north or south to market. Although Hasenclever's aspirations were different from those of Hudson, Middleton or Erkuries Beatty, each of them owed his comfortable affluence to a thriving international economy.

The fighting during the American Revolution, of course, disrupted farming and closed overseas markets. Especially during the campaigns of 1776 and 1778, regular troops and local forces seized cattle and crops for food, destroyed farm buildings and mills, and occasionally terrorized the civilian population.

Cut off from European imports, New Jersey residents had to rely more fully on home manufacturing than in earlier times, and they had to deal with the rapidly depreciating currency issued by the new American government to finance the war. Both during and after the war, the British closed the West Indies to American shipping, blocking one of the principal markets of New Jersey grain and livestock farmers. The most serious losses were the great many deaths from battle and disease among the soldiers. But for those who survived, such hardships were only temporary: the rural economy replenished itself rapidly after the war.

Conclusion

Economists measure the success of an economic system in terms of *per capita growth:* increase in wealth, production or income per person. Growth occurs only if people produce more or if what they produce becomes more valuable. Measured in these terms, there was little if any economic growth in early New Jersey. What economic growth did occur was limited to two periods: the initial burst of farm building in the seventeenth century and the mid-eighteenth century years of rising wheat prices. By and large the average residents lived in 1800 not very differently than they would have in 1700.

But there were far more people in New Jersey at the end of the eighteenth century than there had been at the beginning. That so many more lived as well as earlier generations was a remarkable achievement. Economists designate this *extensive growth.* In Europe, population growth had often brought on famine and plague because there was no land available for expansion; in colonial America, settlers took and worked the land they needed to feed ever more people.

By doing so they brought an end to the agricultural ways of the Lenape. While the replacement of Lenape villages by European farms and towns had numerous consequences, three things illustrate how momentous the change was. First, Europeans cleared the land for crops and timber far more systematically than the Lenape had ever done. With European grain-farming methods they fed more people, but they eradicated the ground cover, depleted the soil, and eliminated much of the wild animal population. Second, they introduced domesticated animals (cows, pigs, sheep, horses) that Native Americans did not have, even further increasing the number of people the agricultural economy could support. Farm animals ate the ground clean and further accelerated soil erosion, and it was not until well into the eighteenth century that the land-rich European-Americans became concerned enough to use animal dung on the soil. Finally, the Europeans were part of an Atlantic market economy. Market-oriented activity produced substantial accumulations of wealth for some settlers at the expense of other newcomers. Slavery, of course, was the most extreme example of this. The contrast between wealth and poverty sharply distinguished European communities from Lenape villages, where gradations of status were seldom marked by the accumulation of goods. New people had truly created a new land.

CHAPTER TWO

Industrialization and the Transformation of the New Jersey Economy, 1800–1920

In August 1795, two judges of the New Jersey Supreme Court, riding circuit in Burlington County, heard the case of *Merritt v. Parker.* Parker owned land on both sides of Rancocas Creek. In about 1780, he had built a dam across the creek and used the dammed-up water to operate a sawmill. In 1793, the New Jersey legislature had passed an act confirming Parker's right to dam the Rancocas. In that same year, Merritt, who owned land on both sides of the creek directly above Parker, had "cut a small trench from the creek, through his own land, by which he conducted a portion of water into a small natural rivulet [or small creek] . . . . to turn the sawmill which he had erected."[1] The rivulet emptied back into the Rancocas by way of a small, uncultivated piece of Parker's lands, and Parker retaliated by blocking it there, backing up water into Merritt's mill so that it could not operate. There were now two dams, two mills, and two angry mill owners facing each other in court.

In 1830, the same court heard a strikingly similar case, this time not between rural mill owners but rather between two corporations, each chartered in the hope of stimulating the economy.

The plaintiff, the Society for Establishing Useful Manufactures, had been created by the New Jersey legislature in 1791. It had bought land around the Great Falls of the Passaic River and built a dam across the river to divert water through a raceway (canal). Then, after attempting to run its own mills, it had leased mill sites to others. The town of Paterson, which had grown up around the society's properties, had a population by 1830 of some eight thousand people, most of them employed in local industry.

In 1824, the legislature had chartered the Morris Canal and Banking Company to construct a canal connecting the Passaic and Delaware rivers. The canal held out the promise both of bringing raw materials from Pennsylvania to industrial sites in northeastern New Jersey and of opening the rural northern part of the state to urban markets. To further its work, the company placed a dam on the Rockaway River, drawing off some of the water that normally ran from it into the Passaic.

This dam significantly reduced the quantity of water available to the Society for Establishing Useful Manufactures. The canal company sought to compensate for the water loss by feeding water from Lake Hopatcong back into the Passaic, but as far as the Society for Establishing Useful Manufactures was concerned, such compensation was not enough. Without a guarantee of a continuous, strong flow of water, mill owners would not want to locate their operations in the Passaic-Paterson area.

How should the court have decided these cases? If the question was fairness, who had the better argument? If the question was maximizing economic benefits, who deserved to win? What interest, if any, did the citizens of New Jersey have in the outcome of each case? Sawmills were, of course, part of the landscape in colonial New Jersey. Virtually every township had one. Did Northampton, where *Merritt v. Parker* originated, need a second mill? Should Parker win the case because he had built first and had served the community since 1780? Or was he simply a self-interested mill owner who was now trying to thwart competition even as the needs of the community grew? How balanced were the equivalent claims of the two companies in the case from 1830? Should the welfare of the manufacturing company prevail over the interests of the canal company? Was the case simply a matter of corporate profit or did it involve the contribution each company might make to the state as a whole?

Thinking about these two cases provides one way of understanding how the nineteenth century differed economically from the eighteenth. Both cases had their origins in entrepreneurial activity: the risking of money in a relatively new endeavor in hopes of profit. In the eighteenth century, most entrepreneurs were merchants and shipowners; in the nineteenth century, most were manufacturers. In both cases, the state of New Jersey was actively promoting economic development. Not only did it provide legal protection for investments, but it also chartered some of the enterprises involved and enabled them to raise funds and use the land and waterways of the state. To be sure, in the eighteenth century government had a role in the economy, although this was generally restricted to setting limits on what people could do (telling inhabitants, for example, how much they could charge for wheat and where they could build bridges or erect fences); in the nineteenth century, the state government enthusiastically committed itself to facilitating improvements in banking, commerce, agriculture, and manufacturing. Finally, both of these cases involved major changes in the landscape. If European settlers transformed New Jersey by turning forested Lenape hunting area into cultivated fields, the entrepreneurs of the nineteenth century radically reshaped the environment again as they built mills, canals, railroads, and cities.

The differences between these two cases tell us something as well about the economy of the nineteenth century. Thirty-five years after *Merritt v. Parker,* the scale of enterprise and the scope of economic endeavor involved in the Morris Canal case had changed strikingly. Now the projects were no longer tied directly to a farming population but were part of a conscious effort to transform the state's economy. Even more striking is how the cases were resolved. In *Merritt v. Parker,* the court, after admonishing both parties for failure to reach a compromise, ruled in favor of the mill operator who built his dam first; the interest he had established by acting first could not be overthrown even, presumably, if the community would benefit from a second mill. In the Morris Canal case, however, the court sidestepped the issue of the Society for Establishing Useful Manufactures' right to the water supply for the Passaic River, and it fashioned a decision that allowed both enterprises to go on about their business. By 1830, economic growth was the goal.

This chapter tells the story of a period of unprecedented economic growth in New Jersey. In Chapter One, we saw how Native American agriculture gave way to European farming. In this chapter, the focus is on how, during the nineteenth century, the growth of a manufacturing economy transformed New Jersey once again. The transformation was revolutionary—fundamental, disruptive, and irreversible—even if ultimately beneficial to most people. Water- and steam-powered machines replaced handwork, and factories and mills took the place of craft shops. Textiles led the way. First in England and then in New England, the spinning and weaving of cotton, wool, and flax into finished products was mechanized. Such manufacturing quickly spread to the middle states, especially Pennsylvania and New Jersey. A process that began with textiles gradually created an *industrial economy.*

To the women and men who lived in New Jersey between 1800 and 1920, industrialization meant more than machines and factories. Industrialization also meant new places to live and new people with whom to live. Cities replaced farms; immigrant workers joined native-born laborers. By the early twentieth century, New Jersey was among the most urban, industrial, and ethnically diverse states in America. Its largest and most important city was Newark, which in 1910 had a population of almost 350,000, an industrial labor force of some 60,000 workers, and a diversified manufacturing economy noted for the smelting and refining of copper as well as for leather goods, foundry and machine-shop products, jewelry, and liquor. Jersey City, the state's second largest city, had an equally diverse industrial economy; its leading industries included slaughtering and meat packing, cigar and cigarette manufacturing, gas production, and steam-railroad repair shops. In both cities, immigrant laborers, primarily from Italy and eastern Europe, composed more than half the early twentieth-century industrial work force.

How did this transformation from a rural and agricultural economy to an urban and industrial economy come about? One way of understanding the process is by examining the histories of two dissimilar manufacturing centers: Paterson and Trenton. Paterson was the most intensely industrial city in New Jersey; a higher percentage of its population worked in manufacturing than in any other city. Trenton's economy was more evenly balanced between manufacturing and other economic concerns. Together, their histories will help illuminate how an industrial economy developed in New Jersey.

A Tale of Two Cities: Paterson and Trenton

Paterson began as the small colonial Dutch farming village of Acquackanonk. In the 1790s, cotton manufacturers came to the village with the hope of using the nearby Passaic River to power their mills. After several false starts textile production took hold, and through the middle of the nineteenth century the city, renamed Paterson, grew in response to the booming production of cotton and woolen wares. In the Civil War era, iron and steel replaced cotton as the most dynamic concerns in the city, and by the 1880s, silk manufacturing had won international recognition for Paterson. Population increased from a mere five hundred people in the mid-1790s to five thousand by the mid-1820s, twenty thousand during the Civil War, and 125,000 by 1910, at the height of Paterson's fame as a silk-producing center.

Because Acquackanonk was located at the Great Falls of the Passaic River, it was an ideal site for harnessing water power to drive gristmills and sawmills. The first to recognize this potential was Alexander Hamilton, secretary of the treasury of the new United States. Hamilton was among the organizers of the Society for Establishing Useful Manufactures—the same corporation that would sue the Morris Canal and Banking Company in 1830—and in 1792, the society, or SUM, acquired a corporate charter from the state of New Jersey to promote the industrial development of Paterson. This was the first of a number of instances in which corporations received favorable treatment from the state government, a practice that became widespread during the nineteenth century (and led to court cases like the one discussed earlier). The charter exempted the SUM from property taxes for ten years, allowed it to raise funds with a lottery, and gave it the power of *eminent domain* (the authority to take private property with just compensation for a public purpose). The SUM built a raceway or canal to channel the Passaic River's water to its mills. It erected sawmills and gristmills, began work on a cotton mill and print shop, and hired skilled English artisans, Irish laborers, and local children.

By 1796, the efforts of the SUM to establish manufacturing enterprises on its own had failed. Profits did not come in quickly enough to cover the costs of starting up the operation. But in the following decades, the raceway, the falls, and the mills brought numerous artisan-entrepreneurs to the town. Thomas Gordon, who published his *Gazetteer of the State of New Jersey* in 1834, graphically described the harnessing of water power that drew such artisans to Paterson:

> A dam of 4½ feet high, strongly framed and bolted to the rock in the bed of the river above the falls, turns the stream through a canal excavated in the traprock of the bank, into a basin; whence, through strong guardgates, it supplies in succession three canals on separate planes, each below the other; giving to the mills on each, a head and fall of about 22 feet. By means of the guardgate, the volume of water is regulated at pleasure, and a uniform height preserved .... The expense of maintaining the dam, canals, and main sluicegates, and of regulating the water, is borne by the company.[2]

The artisans (coopers, blacksmiths, carpenters) who moved to Paterson had skills that allowed them to fashion machinery and use the power of the Passaic River. As entrepreneurs, they were willing to risk what few financial resources they had on the gamble they could manufacture things more quickly and profitably than had been done in the past.

Some came from England, Scotland, and Ireland and brought with them (generally illegally) the designs of British textile machines; others simply fashioned machines on a trial-and-error basis to solve specific problems. The most successful of them built mills that employed hundreds of workers; more typically, they worked in small shops with the help of only two or three laborers. Early Paterson had a patchwork quality to it: alongside the textile concerns stood the smaller shops of carpenters, printers, dyers, food retailers, and the like, which served the growing population of mill hands.

By 1815, there were thirteen cotton mills in Paterson and over two thousand workers in all the town's manufacturing concerns. The 1820 federal census of manufacturing listed fifty-four water-powered looms and 12,624 spindles employed in cotton manufacturing in Essex County, and a local 1821 Paterson census noted nine mills with 12,600 spindles and 663 hands. In 1832, the secretary of the treasury, Louis McLane, reported that there were sixteen mills, 39,926 spindles, and 1,597 hands in Paterson.

By modern standards, Paterson's mills were not large; but in the early nineteenth century, when most goods were produced by blacksmiths and carpenters in their own shops and by farm wives who weaved at home, the mills seemed imposing and their operations appeared diverse and complex. The Paterson firm of Godwin, Clarke & Co. was typical. The firm owned both a water-powered textile mill and a brass and iron foundry where machine tools were fashioned for the mill. Capitalized at $150,000, Godwin, Clarke & Co. imported each year some 225,000 pounds of upland cotton from the South and some six hundred tons of pig iron and four hundred tons of coal from Pennsylvania's Lehigh Valley. It employed 220 men at an average wage of $8 per week, and forty-five girls and twenty-three boys at an average wage of $2.50 per week; it sent finished yarn to weavers in Philadelphia and New York, and sold machinery throughout the United States and even in Mexico.

By the late 1830s, Paterson's position relative to the New England textile industry had begun to erode. Compared to the textile mills in Massachusetts and Rhode Island, Paterson firms were small and undercapitalized, and they did not make the transition to steam power and high-speed looms as readily. But even as cotton manufacturing declined, new industries emerged. The entrepreneur behind the most important new development was a journeyman carpenter, Thomas Rogers.

Rogers came to Paterson in 1812 to work for a mill owner

and helped to establish a firm which spun cotton and built machinery. In 1831 Rogers left that company and set up the Jefferson Works. His skill as a machinist and his knack for business put him at the center of the unfolding industrial revolution in the exciting years of the early 1830s. Not only was the introduction of power looms transforming cotton manufacturing, but a new endeavor, steam railroading, was about to alter America's horse-and-wagon transport system radically.

Between 1832 and 1837, Rogers's firm went from supplying parts to manufacturing locomotives. On October 6, 1837, the *Sandusky,* a six-wheeled, steam-powered engine built by Rogers, made the run from Paterson to New Brunswick and then was sold to the Mad River and Lake Erie Railroad of Ohio. In 1838, seven locomotives were built; in 1854, the number rose to 103. As a letter to a Newark newspaper in 1839 noted, Rogers's engines were at least as good as the English locomotives on which they were modeled. The writer had seen the engine pull twenty-four loaded four-wheeled cars of some 120 tons up a grade of twenty-six feet per mile on a run from Jersey City to New Brunswick. He wrote:

> The average speed on the grade was 24½ miles per hour. This may not be in your estimation anything extraordinary, yet, I consider it a performance worth recording, by way of contrast with . . . [what] occurred on the Liverpool and Manchester Railroad in 1829, only ten years ago. Twenty tons on a level road at the rate of ten miles per hour was then considered wonderful. Astonishing.[3]

Rogers was not alone. Through the middle decades of the century, the metal industries led the way as Paterson became one of the most dynamic industrial cities in the world. In 1850, with a population of 11,000, Paterson had 1,450 people employed in the locomotive, iron goods, and machinery industries; by 1870, with a population of 33,600, employment in the metal industries had risen to 5,300. When the Civil War began, the Rogers locomotive works and its two Paterson competitors were turning out 135 engines annually, and during the boom years of railroad building, 1869 to 1873, some 1,683 locomotives were sold. The Watson Manufacturing Company sold structural steel for the building of New York's Museum

of Natural History and Metropolitan Museum of Art. In the 1880s, the Passaic Rolling Mill manufactured the iron beams used in New York's first elevated trains.

If cotton and iron distinguished the first two phases of Paterson's development, silk highlighted the third. The dominance of silk by 1900 is evident in the census figures (tables 1, 2).

John Ryle was the first to manufacture silk profitably at Paterson. Like many other artisan-entrepreneurs, Ryle was born in England, where as a five-year-old orphan he had gone to work in a silk factory. In 1839, twenty years old and newly arrived in America, Ryle was hired to superintend the establishment of Paterson's first silk factory. Within a decade, the industry Ryle helped found was booming.

The expansion of Paterson's silk industry can be attributed to several factors. In the 1850s, the United States government eliminated the import duty on raw silk while increasing the duty on finished silk products. In 1851, John Benson, a cotton manufacturer with an interest in silk, erected the first steam-powered mill, and in the 1870s, the Phoenix Manufacturing Company introduced power looms, which greatly reduced costs but eliminated jobs for skilled hand-loom weavers. Of equal importance, because it helped expand the market for silk products, was the introduction in the 1870s of the jacquard weaving process that allowed intricate, multicolored patterns to be programmed into power looms through punched cards, much as data cards program some computers today.

In 1860, there were seventeen silk factories in Paterson. The 1880 census takers counted eighty-two establishments, and in 1910, three years before a massive strike disrupted the industry, there were 276 manufacturers employing upwards of twenty thousand workers. In 1909 New Jersey produced plain and fancy broad silks, jacquard silks, ribbons, and other silk products worth $65 million annually, and almost all of these came from

Rogers Locomotive and Machine Works, 1832. *From* The Rogers Locomotive Catalog, 1876, *reprinted by the* NEW JERSEY HISTORICAL SOCIETY *in 1983 and used here with its permission.*

Table 1

The Place of Silk in Paterson Industry, 1900[4]

Occupational Group	Number of Workers
Textiles and clothing	6,200
Iron and steel	2,700
Silk	12,600
Total, three industries	21,500
All manufacturing	29,500

Table 2

Silk Workers in the Labor Force Paterson, 1900[4]

	Percentage Working in Silk
Manufacturing workers	43
Employed persons	27
Population	12

the Paterson area. Paterson was widely known as "Silk City" and commonly called the "Lyons of America" after the French silk center.

Trenton's story is different. The city grew more slowly, never became as fully committed to manufacturing, and long remained the marketing center for a prosperous agricultural hinterland. It was this dual character as an industrial town *and* as a retailing and commercial location that distinguished Trenton's development. Trenton's growth, like Paterson's, began with textiles, spurted forward with iron and steel work at midcentury, and then culminated with specialized products—in this case, pottery and porcelain, not silk. A little town of several thousand people as late as 1830, Trenton had seventeen thousand residents at the outbreak of the Civil War and 120,000 by the 1920s when immigration restriction took effect.

Trenton was laid out in the 1670s at the falls of the Delaware River where Assunpink Creek enters. Initially little more than a sleepy provincial village on the road to Philadelphia, Trenton

Silk ribbon weavers about 1910. *Each woman operated two looms, and each loom wove over forty ribbons at a time. Courtesy* COLLECTIONS OF THE PASSAIC COUNTY HISTORICAL SOCIETY.

struck a Swedish traveler, Peter Kalm, this way when he passed through it in October 1748:

> Trenton is a long narrow town, situated at some distance from the Delaware River, on a sandy plain.... It has two small churches, one for people belonging to the Church of England, and the other for the Presbyterians. The houses are built partly of stone, though most of them are made of wood or planks, commonly two stories high, together with a cellar below the building, and a kitchen underground close to the cellar .... Our landlord told us that twenty-two years ago, when he first settled there, there was hardly more than one house; but from that time on Trenton has increased so much that there are at present nearly a hundred houses .... The inhabitants of the place carried on a small trade with goods which they got from Philadelphia, but their chief income consisted in attending numerous travellers between that city and New York.[5]

In the mid-eighteenth century, Trenton became the site of iron and brick manufacturing and a pottery works, but even in 1834, when the town had 425 dwellings, thirteen taverns, and thirty stores, and the Trenton Water Power Company completed a raceway to provide water power for local enterprise, the most notable industrial features of the state's capital were still sawmills and gristmills similar to those found in the rural countryside. But in that same year, when Thomas Gordon published his *Gazetteer,* he noted that on Assunpink Creek there were several newly built cotton mills with power looms, and he went on to outline the vast potential he envisioned for the town:

> The advantages of this site for manufacturing purposes are perhaps unsurpassed by any [other] in the country. Intermediately situated between the great markets of Philadelphia and New York, 30 miles from the former and 60 miles the latter—surrounded by a rich agricultural country, producing a large surplus quantity of grain of every description, and capable of quadrupling its production—upon a river navigable to the ocean, and for near 250 miles above the falls, flowing through a wide and fertile country, whose products may find a ready market here; having also a feeder of the Delaware and Raritan Canal, . . . the facility of obtaining an abundant and cheap supply of anthracite coal by the river and the Pennsylvania canal, . . . the railroads made, and in progress towards New York and Philadelphia. . . . [It has] a healthy country, abundant and cheap provisions, an adequate supply of laborers, convenience in obtaining raw materials, unfailing power for its manipulation.[6]

The first person fully to exploit Trenton's potential was John A. Roebling. Roebling was born in Germany in 1806, studied at the University of Berlin where he acquired some knowledge of engineering, and emigrated to the United States in 1831 to escape the political and religious restraints of German society. After a brief stint at farming, Roebling went to work in 1837 as a canal engineer for the state of Pennsylvania. At that time, when canal boats had to be pulled over otherwise impassable mountains, massive ropes sewn from hemp were used for the task. Roebling fashioned an alternative rope out of wire that was thinner, less expensive, and more durable. Thus began his career as an industrialist.

Roebling's success depended in large measure on the potential use of wire in railroad bridge construction. Railroads were America's largest industry. Before Roebling entered the field, Charles Ellet had already used wire rather than chain links to build a suspension bridge. In 1844, Roebling put a suspension aqueduct across the Allegheny River; in 1847, he built a suspension bridge over the Monongahela at Pittsburgh, and after moving his factory to Trenton in 1848, he accepted the task that Ellet had abandoned of building a wire suspension bridge over Niagara Falls capable of supporting a railroad train.

To a skeptic who doubted the project's feasibility, Roebling responded this way:

> Total weight of locomotive and train, two hundred and forty-five tons, the vertical impact of which, when moving at a speed of about twenty miles per hour, will not be less than four hundred tons; to this we must add the weight of a number of teams [of horses and wagons] which may happen to be on the bridge at the same time a train is passing; also for a foot of snow.

By adding up these items of weight, and "allowing no less than five times the strength of wire," Roebling claimed he could build a bridge that would safely handle the transit of a surging locomotive. He did.[7]

Roebling found markets for his wire in mining operations, with early developers of electrical equipment, and with the first producers of elevators. But his greatest project was his last. In 1866, he was commissioned to begin work on a mammoth sixteen-hundred-foot suspension bridge to connect Brooklyn and Manhattan in New York City. He died from an injury sustained in the work, but his brother, Washington A. Roebling, a former army engineer, saw the project to completion by 1883. Built at a cost of $15.5 million with a center clearance of 135 feet and a suspended span from tower to tower of almost sixteen hundred feet, the Brooklyn Bridge was evaluated in the May 1883 edition of *Harper's New Monthly Magazine:*

> The bridge itself [is] a remarkable sight [to someone crossing]. . . . Under him is the busy river, the two great cities now made one, and beyond, completing the circuit, villa-dotted Staten Island; the marshes, rivers, and cities of New Jersey stretching to Orange Mountain . . . , the Palisades walling the mighty Hudson.

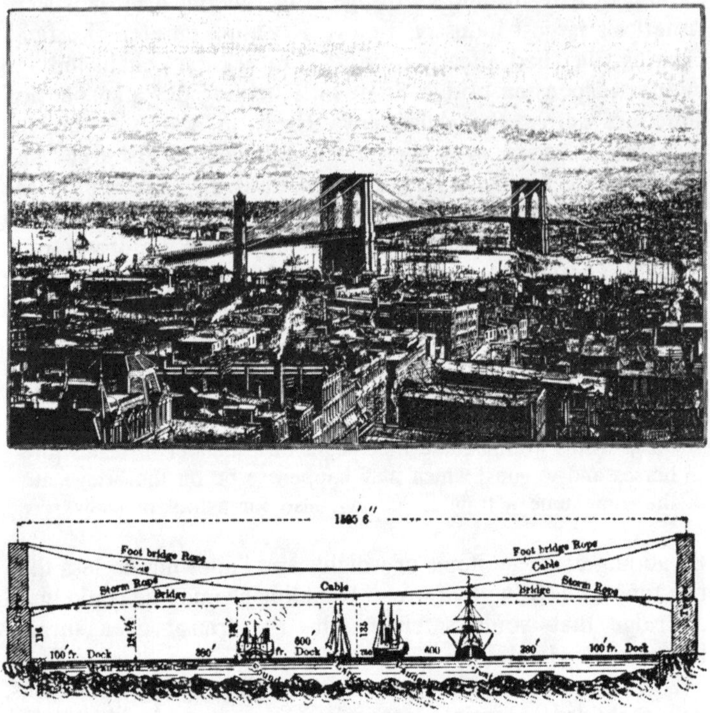

Two nineteenth-century views of the Brooklyn Bridge. *From* Harper's New Monthly Magazine *66 (December 1882–May 1883), 928, 929. The lower figure is an elevation showing temporary ropes that were used in cable making.*

The city now had a landmark, the commentator went on, that dominated its landscape as "St. Peter's from across the Campagna dominates Rome, and the Arc de Triomphe the approach to Paris."[8]

The Roebling iron works, continued by other family members, were part of Trenton's rapid, late-nineteenth-century industrial expansion. The nature of this expansion is summarized in table 3.

Of these industries, none was more closely identified with Trenton than clay working. From the mid-eighteenth century

Table 3

Industrial Growth in Trenton[9]

	Number of Firms	
	1860	1890
Food processing	8	23
Woodworking	21	30
Paper	4	5
Leather	49	7
Iron	23	40
Textiles	7	59
Pottery	10	15
Rubber	2	13
Other	25	69
Total	149	261

on, local clays allowed skilled Trenton farmers to manufacture bricks and coarse red earthenware as a second occupation. By the early nineteenth century, however, Americans began to replace locally made crockery with newer yellow and white earthenware made primarily in England. Production now required multiple, specialized steps (making molds, molding the clay, glazing the crockery, and firing the product in a kiln), and highly skilled laborers, and the midcentury emigration of English potters to Trenton brought the industry to the town. Trenton could offer nearby clays, large markets in Philadelphia and New York, and efficient transportation.

Once established as an earthenware center, Trenton attracted potters with every sort of interest. In 1853, William H. Young, Sr., arrived to manufacture doorknobs of porcelain (costly china made from fine white clay). William Bloor, also English, set up in Trenton in 1863 and later produced the first porcelain art pieces—portrait busts of Abraham Lincoln and Ulysses S. Grant. Walter Scott Lenox, who got his start as a potter's apprentice in Trenton, created a china firm that in 1918 fashioned the dinnerware for Woodrow Wilson's White House. Sanitary plumbing fixtures were added to Trenton's specialties in the 1870s, and bathroom tiles in the 1880s. In 1919, according to census figures, Trenton produced $11.7 million in pottery, about 72 percent of the state total, and nearly five thousand people worked in the industry. The city had won the title of

.. "Staffordshire of America"; like Paterson it had duplicated the success of a famed European manufacturing center.

Why did it happen? What caused the growth of Paterson and Trenton? What caused the even more substantial growth of Newark and Jersey City? By the early twentieth century, what made Perth Amboy a center for copper smelting and refining, Bayonne a leader in oil refining, Camden the site for tanning, currying, and finishing leather, and Elizabeth the home for the manufacture of sewing machines?

There was no single cause. Rather, the industrial transformation of New Jersey, while disruptive and overwhelming, occurred gradually and had many contributing factors. The continuing prosperity of agriculture was crucial because it allowed a limited number of farms to feed a growing urban work force. Also important was the role of New Jersey's state government in encouraging and subsidizing economic growth. The state offered charters (such as the one given the SUM) to entrepreneurs, giving them powers and privileges that enabled them to profit from their enterprises. Profit, in fact, drove the entire economic system. Profit provided the incentive to create, expand, and control economic activity. While each of these factors helped cause industrial transformation, three other factors—immigration, transportation improvements, and technological development—seem particularly crucial to the story of New Jersey's nineteenth-century economy.

Causes of Change: Immigration

Immigrants built New Jersey's industrial economy. The first great wave of postrevolutionary-era immigration carried the English and Irish to the state. The new English immigrants brought experience as weavers and spinners in the textile mills of Manchester and other industrial cities, which served them well in America. Men worked as hand-loom weavers or found industrial jobs, while women and children were engaged as mill workers. Those who came early, or with capital, or with knowledge of how to devise textile equipment or machine tools, often prospered and became manufacturers who induced subsequent immigrants to come.

With the English came the Irish. Before 1840, this group of immigrants included a substantial number of artisans and small

T. C. Alcott and Son, Manufacturer of Turbine Water Wheels and Mill Machinery, Mount Holly, New Jersey. *From J. D. Scott,* New Historical Atlas of Burlington County, New Jersey *(Philadelphia, 1876). Reprinted by the* BURLINGTON COUNTY HISTORICAL SOCIETY, *1991.*

farmers, and a fairly even balance of Catholics and Protestants. The character and volume of Irish immigration was changed markedly by the Irish Poor Law Act of 1838 and the famine of 1845–1849. During the 1850s over a million and a half Irish men, women, and children left their homeland; most were poor Roman Catholic agricultural laborers from southern Ireland.

They provided much of the work force that built New Jersey's railroads and canals, and were drawn disproportionately into the brutal work of the early iron and steel industries. Even more Irish women came than men; they delayed marriage to pursue paid work, and many continued in textiles and domestic labor even after they married, in contrast to native-born women, who left employment after marriage. By 1860, half the state's foreign population was Irish, and the Irish would remain the most numerically significant foreign group in the New Jersey population through the 1880s.

German immigration began later and continued longer than

LIME & HAIR
OFFICE
AND COAL YARD

Irish immigration. In 1860, Germans were the second largest immigrant group in the state, about 33,000 in number. By 1900, they were the largest immigrant group at approximately 120,000. As with the second Irish wave, German immigration was sparked by rural distress during the 1840s. It initially brought Catholic newcomers from southwestern Germany, but later in the century, the balance turned in favor of eastern Germany and of Protestant and Jewish immigrants. German men, like the Irish, settled everywhere and did everything; German women were less likely than Irish women to accept domestic service (despite good pay) and more likely to quit industrial work when they married.

The late nineteenth century is often called the era of the "new" immigration. Between 1891 and 1929, some 22 million new Americans arrived from overseas. The new immigrants came from southern and eastern Europe, especially Italy and Poland; most were Catholic, and a sizable minority were Jewish. Males predominated more than among earlier immigrants. Some, bringing skills from industrial towns in the Italian Piedmont or Eastern Europe, quickly found employment in the silk industry, where they replaced English, German, and native-born workers. Others, the majority, came with only an agricultural background and settled for unskilled employment or exhausting outdoor labor, as had the Irish (table 4).

The open door for immigrants was closed in the 1920s. In 1917, restrictionists in Congress succeeded in imposing a literacy test on immigrants; in 1924, Congress followed with the National Origins Act. Beginning in 1929, annual immigration from each country would be limited to two percent of the number of nationals of that country who had lived in the United States in 1890. The legislators meant to discriminate between "new" and "old" immigration, and, aided by the religious bigotry and political intolerance of the 1920s, they triumphed.

Lumber and Coal Yards of I. W. Heuling's Sons, Centerton, Burlington County. *From J. D. Scott,* New Historical Atlas of Burlington County, New Jersey *(Philadelphia, 1876). Reprinted by the* BURLINGTON COUNTY HISTORICAL SOCIETY, *1991.*

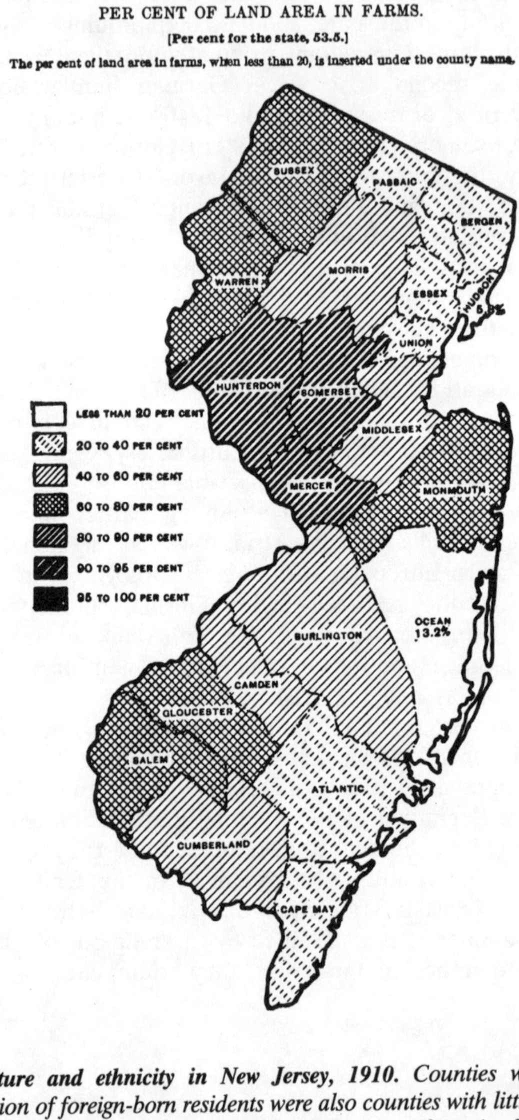

Agriculture and ethnicity in New Jersey, 1910. *Counties with a large proportion of foreign-born residents were also counties with little farmland. A large foreign-born population indicated that manufacturing had replaced agriculture. From United States Census Office,* Thirteenth Census of the United States, 1910, Abstract . . . with Supplement for New Jersey *(Washington, D.C., 1913), pp. 605, 608.*

PER CENT OF FOREIGN-BORN WHITE IN TOTAL POPULATION.

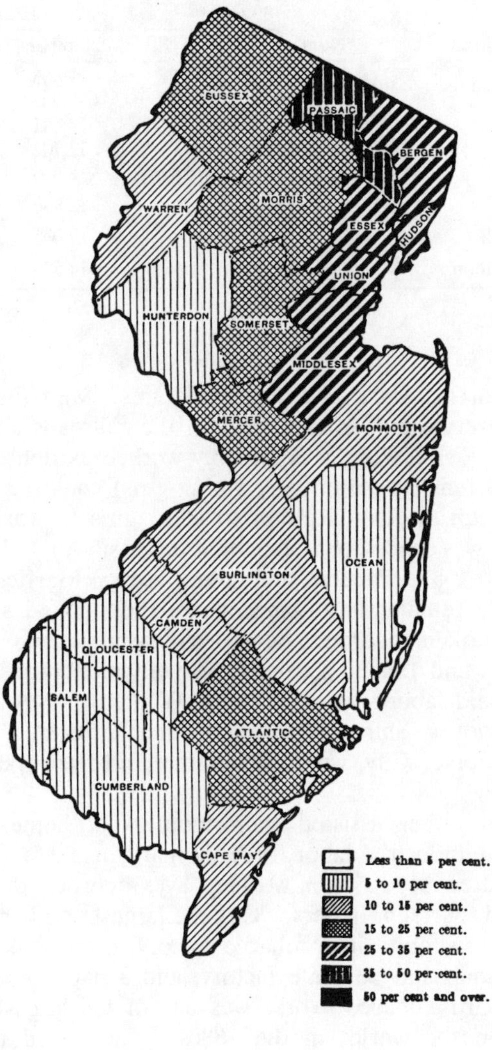

Table 4

Newark's Foreign-born (FB) Population[10]

	1890		1920	
Country of birth	Number	% of FB	Number	% of FB
Italy	2,921	5	27,465	23
Russia	1,295	2	19,969	17
Germany	26,520	48	14,041	12
Poland	463	1	13,702	12
Ireland	13,234	24	8,840	8
All others	11,138	20	32,986	28
Total FB	55,571	100	117,003	100
Total population	181,830		414,524	

What sort of work awaited immigrants? Men found work virtually everywhere: in factories, on the railroads and canals, along the docks. Women commonly worked as domestics, but unmarried females (often very young girls) could be found as well in factories. The decision to allow girls to work outside the home was made from economic necessity or followed the traditions of a particular immigrant group. Married women more often remained at home, where they looked after their families, took in boarders, served as washerwomen, accepted piecework, and tended gardens. For tenement women, some form of paid labor was a necessity. Women in Newark made buttons, gloves, shirts, suspenders, and artificial flowers at home. In Jersey City, women manufactured fireworks in their homes.

Children either assisted their mothers at home tasks or entered the industrial labor force, primarily as factory workers. Most children began their working lives between the ages of twelve and fourteen. In Jersey City the largest numbers of child workers were found in a tobacco factory, a crucible and lead works, a soap and perfume factory, and a paper box factory. The Lorillard Tobacco Works was one of the largest tobacco factories in the world; in the 1880s, it employed thirty-five hundred workers, of whom twenty-five hundred were female, many of them young girls. These youngsters were engaged in a variety of tasks, weighing out tobacco, sorting and stripping it, and putting it up in packages. One part of the process was

Tenement life of immigrant family workers: Children sorting rags gathered by the men. *From* Report of the Board of Tenement House Supervision of New Jersey, 1904, *in* Documents of the One Hundred and Twenty-Ninth Legislature of the State of New Jersey *(Trenton, 1905), 2, between pages 32 and 33.*

described as follows: "One [worker] fills the bags or papers, another seals and ties them, while a third puts on the labels and passes them over to the girl who adjusts the stamp."[11] In a report on child labor, written by the state Bureau of Statistics in 1903 to justify the practice, the short accounts of family work graphically demonstrated the conditions faced by some working families:

> [Case] No. 263, a boy: A large and industrious family consisting of the father, mother, and ten children. The father is idle at present on account of a strike. When all are employed the united income is $35 a week . . . .
>
> No. 269, a girl: Mother, a widow, works in same mill with this child: their joint earnings has to support two other children and an aged grandmother.
>
> No. 290, a girl: Mother a widow; three children—one of whom works. Mother does laundry at home. The earnings of the two support the family.
>
> No. 302, a boy: Mother, a widow, and this boy is the sole support of three younger children.
>
> No. 306, a girl: Father, mother and six children compose the family. Father and three children working; their united earnings support a fairly good home. Children do not attend night school; are too tired to do so.[12]

The bureau concluded its report by arguing that without child labor, many working-class families could not get by; it did not consider the effect of raising the wages paid to adult laborers.

Factory work might bring a family $20 a week, but only if several members worked (table 5). From these wages, the family bought bread at five cents a loaf, meat at twelve cents a pound, and eggs at twenty-five cents a dozen, and then paid rent of about ten dollars per month. Some families spent years in boarding houses and tenements before they could afford their own homes.

The cost of earning these wages was substantial. There was, first, the physical exhaustion of a ten-hour day, six days a week. Strikes closed plants for extended periods of time and left

Table 5

Typical Weekly Wages in the Silk and Iron Industries, 1904[13]

Type of Work	Men	Women
Broad and ribbon silk	$10–12	$6–7
Silk dyeing	$10–12	under $5
Silk throwing	$5–6	$5–6
Structural steel	$10–12	no women

workers without pay. Even in times of industrial peace, workers might find themselves temporarily jobless for several months when plants shut down during periods of slack demand for their goods. There was, beyond that, a significant risk of injury or death on the job, and even when workers avoided injury, factory conditions might do long-term harm to their health. Tuberculosis, rheumatism, and bronchitis were all common illnesses associated with textile and clothing work. The worst conditions were probably found in contract labor done at home in the tenement houses. Artificial flower makers could be identified by the dyes that discolored their fingers. The materials used were toxic and caused the deaths of many youngsters who sat beside or played near their working mothers and innocently put the materials into their mouths.

Nonetheless, immigrants continued to come and eagerly sought any employment that brought twelve dollars a week. Nothing better illustrates this than the situation in Paterson and Trenton. In 1920, some 42 percent of Paterson's population had foreign-born parents and 33 percent were of foreign birth themselves; in Trenton, the corresponding figures were 34 percent and 25 percent. They made the silk ribbons, iron locomotives, and structural steel that brought New Jersey industrial prosperity.

Causes of Change: Transportation Improvements

When George Rogers's first locomotive puffed its way from Paterson to New Brunswick, it helped usher in a new era, a transportation revolution. Trains were the smokiest, noisiest, and most exciting manifestation of the new age. But they were only half the story. At least through the Civil War, canals played an even more important role in accelerating the exchange of bulky goods between city and country. Trains and canals together brought most Americans into a market economy.

No event better symbolized the transportation revolution than the 1825 completion of the Erie Canal. It connected Albany on the Hudson River to Buffalo on Lake Erie and brought all the rich farming land of upstate New York into contact with New York City. During the same period, New Jersey entrepreneurs built two canals.

The Morris Canal was designed to unite the industrial interests of Essex County with the agricultural regions of northern New Jersey and the anthracite coal fields of Pennsylvania's Lehigh Valley. The state refused to finance the project, and investors formed a private corporation to run the canal from the Hudson to the Delaware. Difficult terrain and lack of money delayed completion until 1831, when the first barges were able to make the ninety-eight mile run from Phillipsburg to Newark.

New Jersey's other canal grew out of the long-held dream of connecting Philadelphia and New York City by direct waterway. Private investors launched the project as the Delaware and Raritan Canal and Banking Company (D & R). In 1831, it merged with its rival, the Camden and Amboy Rail Road and Transportation Company. The C & A was one of five railroads chartered by the state in a burst of enthusiasm in 1830–1831, before a single mile of track had been laid anywhere in America. In the spring of 1834, thanks to the labor of Irish immigrants, the D & R opened for trips from Bordentown to New Brunswick.

No two canals could have been less alike. The Morris Canal was over twice as long as the D & R and negotiated a rise and fall of 1,700 feet. The D & R Canal was flat and much wider, and it handled three times the traffic. The D & R was expected to make a profit, and it did through 1900; it was closed in 1933. The Morris Canal, on the other hand, had to revitalize the northern New Jersey economy before its tolls could produce profits. But the canal did not greatly benefit the economy, and the profits never materialized. The Morris Canal did move significant quantities of coal and iron, but by the 1860s, railroad service was quicker (eight hours, not five days, across the state) and more dependable (ice closed the canal in winter). Business dropped off beginning in the 1870s, and in 1919 the state closed the canal.

When the Morris Canal opened in 1831, American railroads were little more than a dream of duplicating early English success at mounting a steam engine on wheels, directing it along tracks, and using it to pull people and cargo short distances. The Camden and Amboy sent its chief engineer, Robert L. Stevens, to England, where he purchased an engine, the *John Bull,* and negotiated a contract to have T-rails of his own design built in Wales. The *John Bull* made its first experimental run on a short strip of track at Bordentown in 1831. By the fall of 1832, track had been laid from Bordentown to Hightstown (the journey to the Atlantic had to be completed by stage); by early 1833, tracks reached South Amboy; and in September, the *John Bull* made its first trip across the state. On its return, the train hit a hog, decapitated it, and fell off the rails. (The engine can be seen today in the Smithsonian Institute.)

Seven years later, in 1840, the C & A was running trains from Philadelphia over a strengthened train bridge at Trenton and then on to the Hudson River. The company had invested over three million dollars in rolling stock, steamboats, and land, and owned seventeen locomotives, sixty-seven passenger cars, and seventy-two freight or baggage cars. It also had eight steamboats to assist in connections across the Delaware and Raritan rivers. Before the Civil War, the railroad generally carried people, not cargoes—some 165,000 people in 1838 and almost half a million by 1860. In 1850, the line introduced commutation tickets for regular riders.

The financial success of the C & A depended not only on its ability to move commuters, but also on the monopoly rights over the New York–Pennsylvania traffic that had originally been granted to it (and the D & R) as a way of attracting investors. The company repeatedly entered New Jersey politics to hold on to this monopoly against the claims of turnpike and steamship concerns, rival railroads, and angry out-of-state investors (who were prohibited from serving on the C & A). And state laws shielded the railroads from full liability for the maiming of pedestrians or damage to private property. More positively, the C & A prospered because it stimulated growth along its route. Bordentown, which was served by both rail and canal service, provides one example of how the C & A helped transform the New Jersey countryside along its route. Thomas Gordon, in his 1834 *Gazetteer,* wrote that Bordentown was a

town of "about 1,000 inhabitants, 200 dwellings . . . , 5 stores and 5 taverns. . . ."[14] In 1871, William Sipes's descriptive survey of the towns served by the Pennsylvania Railroad captured the story of Bordentown's growth.

> The business of the city is active and increases rapidly. It is noted for its institutions of higher learning,—particularly those for females,—among which are a college and several seminaries. Steamboats connect it with Philadelphia in the summer months, and it is a popular place of resort and temporary residence. . . . Among the most prominent industries of Bordentown are a forge, a foundry, a sash factory, saw and flour mills, a shipyard, and a carriage factory. An extensive business is done in dry goods, groceries, and lumber. It contains seven churches, an opera house, two public halls, a bank, and four good hotels. Population, 6,041.[15]

Success finally caught up with the C & A. In 1867, under increasing pressure to provide more efficient freight transport across the state, the C & A merged with its chief rival, the New Jersey Railroad, and in 1871 the new company leased its holdings, at exceptionally good terms, for 999 years to the Pennsylvania Railroad, which was rapidly expanding into a national concern and systematically gobbling up feeder lines and competitors. By 1900, the Penn system owned 486 miles of track and canal in New Jersey, carried 20 million passengers and 26 million tons of freight, and took in $27 million in gross revenues. In the state as a whole, there were some sixteen hundred miles of track, operated by over a hundred companies.

Causes of Change: Technological Development

In Thomas Rogers's development of better crankshafts for locomotives and in John Roebling's improvement of wire rope, technological ingenuity played a role in industrial development. Even more than the careers of Rogers and Roebling, Thomas

Canal and railroad passing next to the Roebling Iron Works, late-nineteenth-century Trenton. *Courtesy* FREE PUBLIC LIBRARY, TRENTON.

A. Edison's life illustrates the relationship between technology, entrepreneurship, and economic development. Edison was born in 1847 in Milan, Ohio. He received little formal education, and at age fifteen learned telegraphy. Telegraphy, simple as it seems today, was *the* most vital and sophisticated technologically dependent concern in America. Telgraph lines not only connected business establishments and financial markets, but also kept the nation's largest business, the railroads, running on schedule. By 1861, telegraph lines spanned the continent.

Edison's early work at transcribing Morse code for newspapers gave him time to tinker; a job with Western Union opened his eyes to telegraph journals, with their stories on inventions and experiments (the equivalent of modern computer magazines). When he made the jump from employee to inventor, he correctly sensed that the highly competitive telegraph market would serve him well. Between 1868 (when he was twenty-one) and 1876, Edison devised a printing-and-dial telegraphy system and an improved method for high-speed transmission of wire messages. He recruited skilled machinists to work with him, found investors willing to underwrite his research, and built a laboratory in Newark.

His break came in 1876. Realizing the threat that Edison's inventions posed, Western Union, the most important telegraph concern in America, gave him a five-year contract. Edison used the funds from this contract and the profits from telegraphy inventions to build a large research lab in Menlo Park. In 1878, additional backing from Western Union stockholders, including J. P. Morgan (already the wealthiest financier in the world) allowed Edison to enlarge the Menlo Park facility and recruit a research team of seventy or more people. It was here that his work on the telegraph, phonograph, telephone, and incandescent lamp went forward. In 1887, Edison completed a new laboratory in West Orange, the largest research and development laboratory of its time; in West Orange, he began work on motion pictures, storage batteries, and ore milling while continuing his development of the electric light and the phonograph.

Edison spent only part of his life in the workshop. He understood patent law, publicity and marketing. His ability to dramatize his inventions and distribute them broadly and profitably helped his career as much as his inventiveness did.

Thomas Edison at work in his chemical laboratory, West Orange, about 1888. *Courtesy* U.S. DEPARTMENT OF THE INTERIOR, NATIONAL PARK SERVICE, EDISON NATIONAL HISTORIC SITE, WEST ORANGE.

As the level of mathematical and engineering skills required in the lab increased, Edison recruited college graduates from Princeton University and Stevens Institute of Technology, where new scientific curricula were available. Late in the century, with math and engineering continuing to increase in complexity, Edison abandoned work on electricity for problems in mechanical and chemical technology.

Thomas A. Edison helped create a world of which he was never fully a part. He had been a businessman, an engineer, and an inventor, and in each capacity he had been self-trained. By the time he left electrical work, technology had became a profession, requiring specialized skills and a division of labor. Colleges trained engineers; ongoing, fully funded research labs became the norm. Marketing departments replaced the flamboyant efforts of the individual inventor to bring a product to the public's attention. Each change helped sustain the consumer economy of the twentieth century that Edison's work had helped create.

Conclusion

Industrialization brought unprecedented economic growth to nineteenth-century New Jersey. Output per capita and output per worker both increased steadily. Industrialization made workers more productive. This was true in manufacturing as well as in agriculture. New Jersey was, by the late nineteenth century, one of the most heavily industrialized and economically various states in America.

Was this progress? If our measure is whether people in 1920 had achieved a better standard of living than people in 1800, then the answer is unquestionably yes. But if we return to the questions asked in the introduction about the consequences of economic growth, then we must qualify our answer somewhat. Consider three of these consequences.

What did industrialization mean to Paterson and Trenton? Paterson industrialized more fully and grew more rapidly; late in the nineteenth century, it soared to prosperity by specializing in silk. Its strength in the nineteenth century eventually became a weakness. When the silk industry declined, so did Paterson. Trenton, in contrast, had a more diversified if somewhat less prosperous economy. As a center for marketing and as New Jersey's capital, the city was better prepared to withstand the shift in America's twentieth-century economy from manufacturing to service activities (these trends are discussed more fully in Chapter Three).

There is as well the question of how the rewards of economic growth were distributed. The commercial economy of the eighteenth century produced increasing inequality. So did the industrial economy of the nineteenth century. Entrepreneurs, who had risked their money to build new, but small businesses, lost out to capitalists, who bought and sold companies as if they were commodities, and who gained monopolistic control over every aspect of the production process, from the supply of raw materials to the distribution of the final product. This capitalist reorganization of the economy created corporations of unprecedented wealth, such as John D. Rockefeller's Standard Oil Company of New Jersey and J. P. Morgan's Pennsylvania Railroad (which bought out the Camden & Amboy). Inequality was even more visible in the contrast between the tenement houses of silk operatives and the Victorian mansions of the mill owners. Was this inequality greater than in 1800? Perhaps, but it was also different because the power which wealth bestowed in 1900 was more far-reaching and less subject to government control. Erkuries Beatty, the Princeton farmer we met in Chapter One, was a man of property and standing; he had, in fact, served as an officer in the Revolutionary War, and in the 1790s, he was a justice of the peace in the county government. Yet it would be difficult to call him powerful. He was almost as dependent on the field hands he hired as they were on him—they needed the work, but other farmers would hire them; he needed their labor or his crop would go to waste. Contrast Beatty with the men who ran the Camden & Amboy Rail Road. They hired hundreds of workers, secured a monopoly from the state on the most prosperous rail route in America, and used both the court system and the legislature to protect themselves from competition and irate consumers. The economic and political power of corporations like the Camden & Amboy, or like the Roeblings of Trenton, dwarfed that of prosperous rural notables of the colonial era.

Finally, there is the problem of waste. When the first mill was built and the first railroad run, the benefits seemed clearly to outweigh the cost. Disturbing a farmer's quiet enjoyment of his or her property seemed a small price to pay for the obvious advantages of better marketing and transportation. But if one landowner could profit from a mill on Rancocas Creek, then a second one was likely to try, and the courts had cases such as *Merritt v. Parker* to resolve. By midcentury the river that had supported one mill now had dozens, and the county that had had one railroad now had many. The government promoted this growth, but neither planned nor regulated it. Entrepreneurs dotted New Jersey's landscape with new industrial ventures, many of which would fail in the competition of the marketplace. This was, perhaps, creative destruction, as the new replaced the old, but such growth also destroyed much of the physical beauty and human endeavor of an earlier New Jersey.

Epilogue: Continuity or Change?

John Ten Eyck lived and farmed along the Raritan River in the mid-nineteenth century not far from where, half a century before, Erkuries Beatty had lived. His diary is an ordinary recounting of the routines of rural life in Somerset County:

> *Dec. 27, 1855* [Winter]
> This morning I took the car [train or coach] and went to Somerville, I got a gallon of lamp oil of C. Barcalow and paid him $1.25 for it. I bought a pair of brick skin gloves lined for 10/. After dinner John Cox came with his machine and we threshed off 2 runnings of clover off the straw.
>
> *April 25, 1856* [Spring]
> This morning I took 50 bushels of oats to the depot for B. B. Smith; he paid me 17 dollars for it this forenoon. I went to Raritan; I paid Dunkem 8 dollars on the corn sheller that I got of him. I took my policy of insurance with me; I left it with John A. Steats. . . . He said if the buildings got burned down before I got my policy, we would become responsible for the insurance. This forenoon John Van Derbuk came and got 8 bushels of potatoes of me; he paid me $4.62 for them. This afternoon, I plowed in the upper orchard for corn.
>
> *July 5, 1856* [Summer]
> This morning William Smith, Garret Conover, Abraham Burnhart, Serinus T. Stryker helped me and Irish Michael in harvest to day. Stryker worked for me to pay for my hands helping him cut 2 loads of hay and drawing it home for him. We cut wheat with three cradles until noon. Cornelius Hall came with his machine and cut wheat for me. We finished the wheat

at 5 o'clock and after tea he cut rye with the machine until sunset. I paid Irish Michael 50 cents to pay for his clothes being washed.

September 11, 1856 [Fall]

This morning Dutch James commenced to work for me by the month; he came with Dutch Jacob from New York last evening. This morning had Dutch James spread lime. This morning I went to Newark to the State agricultural fair. I went with the cars. . . . I got home this evening at 8 o'clock.[16]

John Ten Eyck's diary records a life much like that of Erkuries Beatty. The industrial transformation of New Jersey seemingly had had little impact on the day-to-day activities of the farming population. Farmers still regulated their activities according to nature: the day ran from sunup to sunset and the work required to keep the farm going still depended on the seasonal demands of plowing, sowing, and harvesting. Unlike mill and factory owners, farmers did not hire large numbers of full-time laborers to do their work, but depended on their own families, part-time help to help with particular tasks, and the assistance of friends when a task had to be done quickly. They carried their own crops to the market, and they sold a little bit here and a little bit there to neighbors, just as they bought some of what they needed from other farmers and grew and fashioned much of what they wanted at home.

Yet in other ways, Ten Eyck's diary records the subtle intrusions on rural life of the urban, industrial world. He carried his crop to a "depot," probably a train stop, rather than by cart to Trenton as Beatty had done. He used threshing machines, whereas Beatty did all his work with simpler tools, and he as often referred to clock time as to the sun in describing his day (not only did this represent a new, more systematic way of thinking about time, but it also reflected the fact that farmers now commonly owned watches, whereas in the late eighteenth century they rarely had). He owned an insurance policy on his barn, and at least one of his laborers had come from Ireland, part of the nineteenth-century mass migration that brought Old World workers to the urban, industrial economy of the New World. More generally, other parts of the diary reveal a knowledge of the larger world—of foreign events and American politics—and an ease of movement—to Newark, to Trenton, to Philadelphia—uncommon in Beatty's era when both transportation and communication were far slower.

John Ten Eyck was not a representative figure of his age. Farmers and farm laborers no longer made up the majority of the population. But in the late 1850s, when Ten Eyck wrote his diary, there were still almost as many farmers and farm laborers in the state as manufacturing workers. The persistence of the farming economy was an indication, even as industry transformed New Jersey, of continuity with the past, just as small changes in the day-to-day activities of farmers provide an index of how the new, industrial economy reached out and affected the lives of everyone.

CHAPTER THREE

The Pleasures of Consumption and the Persistence of Poverty: The Economy We Live With Today

In May 1932, Katherine Schaub published her story in *Survey Graphic* magazine.[1] To a public accustomed to the notorious and extravagant personalities of the 1920s and now grimly facing the Great Depression, she must have seemed an insignificant individual, but Katherine's narrative had a tragic urgency to it. She started work in 1917, a girl of fifteen who found well-paid employment in the Orange, New Jersey, factory of the U.S. Radium Corporation. The United States had just entered World War I and business was good. Her job was to paint the numbers and hands of watches with a luminous substance that made the watch parts glow in the dark. The company sent some of the watches to American troops in Europe and sold others at home. Katherine dabbed a mixture of water, paste, and radium powder on the watches, and each day after hours of sitting at a table tediously painting watches, she returned home with little spots on her skin, clothing, and hair that glowed in the dark.

In 1921, the war over, Katherine lost her job. Six months later, her cousin Irene, who had worked with her, became mysteriously ill, and in 1923, after a protracted and gruesome struggle, she died. That winter, Katherine began having trouble with her teeth; in 1924, a New York doctor, who had treated another radium worker, told Katherine he thought her jaw infection might be related to her handling of radium. But Katherine didn't die until 1933. Though she was increasingly debilitated, she lived to file suit in 1927 against the company and to begin a book detailing her experiences. Others were not so lucky.

In the early 1920s, neither doctors nor public health officials were generally aware of the dangers of radium. Radium necrosis—more simply, jaw rot—was not covered by insurance laws, and, in any case, the U.S. Radium Corporation denied until the late 1920s that contact with radium was in any way dangerous. The Harvard University investigators called in by the company to study the dangers of working with radium initially gave U.S. Radium a clean bill of health, and the New Jersey Department of Labor refused to become involved until pressured by Katherine Wiley of the National Consumers League. Katherine Schaub eventually won an out-of-court settlement that covered her mounting medical bills, but the statute of limitations protected the company from further suits, and its eventual move to New York ended whatever efforts New Jersey might have made to police the situation.

Katherine Schaub's story should remind us of one underlying theme of this book: economic progress came at a substantial cost, and often without much consideration of other means less threatening to human health or to the environment. These costs, although often great, were difficult to measure in the same terms as profit and loss. Some costs were quite visible, such as the toll industrial accidents took of nineteenth-century immigrant workers. In some cases, the price of progress was hidden; the bill was presented years later. Schaub's illness and the effects of lead poisoning from the unregulated, early twentieth-century use of ethyl gasoline in the first automobiles were two examples. Some costs were invisible, such as the absence of most large game animals from New Jersey's woodlands after European settlers cleared and farmed these animals' natural habitat. These costs should be kept in mind as we turn to New Jersey's modern economy. This chapter will emphasize three themes in the development of that economy: (1) the relative decline of the manufacturing sector of the economy; (2) the rapid growth of the service sector of the economy and with that growth the increasing employment of women and minorities; and (3) the growing importance of consumer spending in fueling economic growth. New Jersey's modern economy has been relatively prosperous, and it has seemed to most of those involved to be self-evidently beneficial; but it is also an economy that has failed to solve the problems of poverty, waste, and pollution associated with economic growth.

An Overview: The New Jersey Economy in 1920

In 1920, the shape of New Jersey's economy was still clearly the product of the industrial development of the nineteenth century: the population was growing rapidly, immigrants made up a sizable portion of the work force, and manufacturing dominated the economy. The state's population, which had been only 211,149 when the nineteenth century began, and 672,035 when the Civil War broke out, had reached 3,155,900 by 1920. Of these almost one-quarter were immigrants and more than a third more were the children of immigrants. The state's occupational structure in 1920 indicated the continuing importance of manufacturing (table 6).

Farmers still used half the available land in New Jersey, but farm families made up less than five percent of the people in the state. From the agricultural census of 1920, the value of farm produce can be estimated at approximately $118 million, but the output of manufacturing was worth $3.7 billion.

The state's urban-industrial character was most evident in the five cities with populations of over 100,000 residents: Newark (with 414,524); Jersey City (with 298,103); and Paterson, Camden, and Trenton. In terms of both employment and the value of production, the largest industry was shipbuilding,

Table 6

Employment, 1920[2]

Occupation	Percentage
Agriculture	4.7
Clerical work	11.6
Domestic work	8.0
Manufacturing	48.0
Mining	.3
Professions	5.3
Public service	2.6
Trade	8.7
Transportation	8.5

spurred on by wartime demand for new vessels. In 1919, some 180 vessels of over five tons were constructed in the state; 107 in Newark alone, and 41 more in Camden and Elizabeth. The silk industry was the second largest, employing some thirty-two thousand workers in almost seven hundred firms. More generally, the textile trades—including not only silk manufacturing, but also makers of cotton and woolen goods—employed more than seventy-one thousand children, women, and men. Ranked behind shipbuilding and silk, in terms of employment figures, were electrical machinery, foundry and machine-shop products, iron and steel works, worsted goods, dyeing and finishing of textiles, chemicals, rubber, and phonographs. This industrial base was New Jersey's most tangible economic link with the past (for details, see Chapter Two).

The year 1920, however, also seemed to Americans a moment of transition to something new. World War I had ended. The war had not only cost American lives, but it had apparently brought to a close two decades of social reform (the "Progressive Era") by refocusing the attention and the energy of Americans on the fighting in Europe. At home, the Red Scare—a systematic effort to suppress political radicals and labor organizers—and the imposition of immigration restrictions marked a new period of intolerance in American life. For the economy, these events had three implications.

First, the Progressive Era practice of increasing government regulation of the economy came to an end. In the early nineteenth century, New Jersey's government had been actively involved in helping to stimulate economic growth, and entrepreneurs, such as those who laid out Paterson and those who constructed the Camden & Amboy Rail Road, welcomed government assistance. After the Civil War, when railroad and manufacturing interests were far better established, large business concerns had less need for direct government assistance and became increasingly wary of the use of government power to regulate business practices and the working conditions of laborers. Under pressure from politically powerful business concerns, state government did little in the late nineteenth century to control the way industrialists and railroad owners ran their businesses. During the Progressive Era, a period associated particularly with Woodrow Wilson's term as New Jersey's governor and with the presidencies of Theodore Roosevelt and Wilson, this trend was reversed. The government regulated banking, the power of corporations, the processing of food, the conditions under which men, women, and children labored, and numerous other aspects of economic life. In public, business leaders opposed regulatory legislation as mere meddlesome interference with free enterprise, but this legislation was often shaped in part by these business leaders and frequently worked to the benefit of established corporations. Nonetheless, business welcomed a return in 1920 to less active state and federal government involvement in the economy. Government, it must be emphasized, did not stop assisting business (for example, through tariff laws and assistance in developing overseas markets), but little new regulatory legislation was passed during the 1920s.

Second, the immigration restrictions of 1920 abruptly and greatly reduced the supply of inexpensive industrial labor. Moreover, child labor legislation passed during the Progressive Era curtailed the use of children in manufacturing. In the short run, the most important consequence of these developments was to encourage some businesses, especially textile producers, to move to the South. Labor costs were lower there because child labor legislation had been defeated and because politicians and business owners manipulated racial tensions to thwart unionizing efforts and keep wages low. In the long run, the restrictions of 1920 meant that new workers came not from European immigration, but from natural (reproductive) population growth, migration into the state from other regions (especially the South), immigration from the Caribbean (particularly Puerto

Rico), and the fuller utilization of underemployed residents, especially blacks and women.

Third, and least tangibly, 1920 witnessed a change in attitude toward economic life. For many, the twenties were a decade not only of seemingly endless prosperity, but also of unabashed efforts to gratify personal desires—a decade of eager consumption. Of course, people had been buying consumer goods throughout the nineteenth century, and for that matter, for centuries, but such purchases were usually justified as necessities, treasured as luxuries, or questioned as wasteful extravagances. The Victorian culture of white Protestant Americans had emphasized hard work, thrift, and self-denial. In the twentieth century, such attitudes handicapped the economy. As manufacturers shifted from making equipment and machinery for government and business to making items for household and personal use, they had to encourage ordinary people to spend and not save their disposable income. Increasing the market for consumer goods, then, required not only economic improvement (more spending income) but also a change in cultural values from self-denial to self-indulgence. In 1920, with the enthusiasm for reform dampened and the war behind them, Americans seemed ready to accept their role as consumers.

Household Appliances and Frivolous Pleasures: the Birth of a Consumer Society

The nineteenth-century industrial revolution created a new middle class, and the middle class created a consumer society. The middle class included the prosperous farmers whose produce fed the urban immigrants, the lawyers and bankers who served the needs of a manufacturing economy, and the employers whose factories dotted New Jersey's landscape. Most of all, the middle class were the small retail dealers, the salesmen and saleswomen, the teachers, and the clerks who made their living from trade, clerical work, or at professions (and who by 1920 accounted for one quarter of New Jersey's employment). Most were white, most were Protestant, and most were native-born. Although not rich, they had money to spend on new conveniences, occasional luxuries, and frivolous pleasures. After World War II, the new buying patterns the middle class established began to be adopted by workers as well. As they spent their earnings, they created a *consumer economy,* that is, an economy based on the gratification of an ever-increasing demand for products to make life more comfortable and enjoyable. What was new in the twentieth century was not the purchase of consumer goods—this, as already noted, had been going on for centuries—but rather the significance of consumer spending for economic growth and the extent to which business encouraged and ordinary people enjoyed buying consumer goods.

No change in consumption patterns was more noticeable than the reshaping of the household economy. Over the course of the nineteenth century, the traditional tasks of producing food and clothing, which had long been done at home, moved out of the household; families became consumers as well as producers. The household lost its role in producing for the market, but not its role in production. Meals had to be prepared, clothing repaired, cleaning done, and firewood secured; if anything, the sheer drudgery of housework increased and fell exclusively on women. In the late nineteenth and early twentieth centuries, indoor plumbing and then electrification transformed the household once again (table 7). Piped-in water eliminated tedious trips to draw well water or use an outdoor privy but increased the amount of cleaning that had to be done in the home; electric washing machines eliminated hand cleaning, but increased the pressure to launder everything; the vacuum cleaner decreased the stooping required to clean a house, but not the "necessity" to clean; the refrigerator made it easier to

Table 7

Improvements and Appliances in Thirty-Six Medium-Sized American Cities, 1927[3]

	Homes (%)
Electricity	97
Plumbing	93
Gas ranges	80
Vacuum cleaners	60
Electric washers	29
Iceless refrigeration	2

store food, but committed people to endless trips to buy prepared foods. With a range of home appliances at her disposal, the middle-class, twentieth-century housewife might escape the grinding physical exhaustion that poorer women faced, but she worked even longer than she had before. And, she began to sense that others measured her worth by how well she managed the appliances that manufacturers encouraged her to buy.

Perhaps even more dramatic was the way the automobile rearranged American life. First produced for sale in the late 1890s, automobiles were sold to four thousand Americans in 1900, 187,000 in 1910, 1.5 million in 1921, and over 5 million by 1929. Henry Ford, after establishing the Ford Motor Company in 1903, produced over 15 million Model T's (Tin Lizzies) between their introduction in October 1908 and their discontinuance in May 1927. By that time, perhaps three out of every five American homes had a car, and virtually everyone *wanted* one (this demand for new products being one of the distinguishing features of a consumer economy). Cars transformed the way Americans lived and worked; their availability helped reorganize shopping (people drove to buy goods rather than had them delivered), and shifted to middle-class mothers the burden of transporting food and children. Their production stimulated young industries and provided new markets for older businesses (Trenton's rubber industry, for example, benefited from the new demand for automobile tires and tubing). Their convenience created new forms of leisure and new leisure industries, as we shall see in the case of the New Jersey beaches, which became marketable when they could be reached easily by large numbers of people who lived some distance away.

The use of leisure was, in fact, the most conspicuous indication of the new middle-class desire for consumption, and so it is worth spending some time exploring how leisure became a product sold by a new set of industries. Nothing so clearly symbolized the birth of a consumer society in New Jersey as the creation of Atlantic City. Atlantic City was originally the dream of Richard B. Osborne, a Philadelphia businessman and engineer. In 1854, Osborne, with the backing of like-minded manufacturers from New Jersey and Pennsylvania, ran a train line from Camden to Absecon Island, where a year later Atlantic City was incorporated. Atlantic City was to be the resort for

Philadelphia's newly affluent middle class. Osborne's railroad would carry them to the ocean, where his agents would sell them beachfront property or dine and bed them in oceanfront hotels that he and his partners owned. Osborne's plan did not work out, and a bloody Civil War turned the country's attention elsewhere, but better days were ahead.

In 1870, Atlantic City was home to a mere thousand people; by 1920, the population was over fifty thousand. These were the resort's boom years. The first boardwalk was built in 1870. By 1896 this crude structure had been replaced with a four-mile-long, forty-foot-wide, electrically lit boardwalk. In 1876, the Philadelphia and Atlantic City Railway provided a second line to Pennsylvania, and soon after that a rail connection to New York City was completed. By 1888, there were more than five hundred hotels and boardinghouses to lodge the thousands of weekend beachgoers these trains brought to Atlantic City.

In 1882 Colonel George W. Howard constructed the first public amusement pier. Other, larger ones followed, with evocative names like Heinz Pier, Steel Pier, and Auditorium Pier. So did the most exciting machine-powered amusements of the century: the Ferris wheel, the merry-go-round, and the "flip flap railway" (an early roller coaster that carried two people in a small train car around the interior of a vertical, twenty-five-foot-high circle of track). Atlantic City was boisterous, exciting, and crude. A quick ferry ride across the Delaware and an hour-and-a-half excursion through the Pine Barrens of central New Jersey, and the train abruptly and noisily deposited the vacationer in sight of the ocean, among magnificent hotels that rose from the sand as if Atlantic City were an oasis. Left behind were the squalor and routine of the industrial city. Here seemingly endless pleasure—innocent and not-so-innocent—were available: games along the boardwalk, carriage rides on the beach (horse manure became a problem), and

Beach and boardwalk at Atlantic City, around 1875. *From Edwin Shinn,* A Century After: Picturesque Glimpses of Philadelphia and Pennsylvania *(Philadelphia, 1875), p. 70. Courtesy ATLANTIC COUNTY HISTORICAL SOCIETY.*

vaudeville shows "suited for the whole family," as well as three times as many taverns per person as in New York City, illegal gambling houses, and prostitution (eventually restricted to particular areas of town).

The sexes could mingle more freely and dress less discreetly than was customary in Victorian America, and social distinctions were harder to maintain in the casual give-and-take of the boardwalk. In an era of racism, the city was one of the few places to offer blacks substantial employment opportunities (primarily as cheap domestic labor in the hotel business), and a place where black vacationers could find some relief from the segregation that met them virtually everywhere else. This was not America without rules, but with rules relaxed; in any case, it was over in a weekend and the worker went back to the realities of urban life, factory labor, and wage dependence—of being a cog in the machine of production.

Leisure, in a culture that worshiped technology and made Thomas A. Edison a folk hero, was as much a product of science as it was a result of the commercialization of the Atlantic City beaches. In the last decade of the nineteenth century, science brought the movies to American culture. The first movies were pathetically crude, and once their novelty wore off, they routinely bored the vaudeville audiences who sat through them. Flickering, disjointed images that lasted little more than a minute, scenes with little action (boxing matches were the exception), and uninteresting characters flawed the early efforts. The competition to develop and improve moving pictures was intense, however, and New Jersey, because of the presence of Edison's West Orange laboratory, was at the center of this competition. In the early 1890s, Edison and his assistant, William Kennedy Laurie Dickson, exhibited a "kinetoscope machine" that allowed a single viewer to see a one-minute film through a peephole. Edison patented a coin-operated kinetoscope in 1893, established a makeshift studio known as the "Black Maria," and financed viewing parlors nationwide.

For all of the inventor's technical brilliance, the key to business success was the partnership with artistically talented camera operators and producers and with distributors and theater owners who could pull in the public. Edison's greatest success came when he teamed with cameraman Edwin S. Porter, who in 1903 shot *The Great Train Robbery* using the Erie and

Theda Bara in "Romeo and Juliet." *Courtesy the* *MUSEUM OF MODERN ART/FILM STILLS ARCHIVE, NEW YORK.*

Lackawanna Railroad lines near the Passaic River as a setting.

The first decades of the twentieth century witnessed a proliferation of little production studios and an outpouring of films. While most companies were based in New York City, many ferried their film crews across the Hudson to use New Jersey settings for their movies. New Jersey supplied more natural surroundings than the teeming streets of the city for the adventure tales of cowboys and pirates that dominated early cinema. Using the imposing backdrop of the Palisades, a director could design a fantasy that transported audiences to almost any place or time.

Among the early film makers, one of the best known was William Fox. The child of Jewish immigrants, Fox began with a penny arcade, built a chain of movie houses, and then in 1914 branched into filmmaking. He established Willat Studios in Fort Lee and additional movie sites in Jersey City, Hoboken,

Cliffside and Grantwood. Before the decade was out, Fox would be lured by the sunshine of southern California and leave New Jersey for Los Angeles. There he would create Twentieth Century Fox.

With the multiplication of consumer industries came new, increasingly sophisticated means of marketing products. In fact, retailing and wholesaling became more significant than actual production in terms of employment and revenue. This development, one of the basic characteristics of New Jersey's consumer economy, was clearly reflected in the rise of the department store. In the late nineteenth century, Newark, the state's leading commercial center, had three: Hahne's (founded in 1858), L. S. Plaut's (1870), and Bamberger's (1892).

Department stores provided consumers an alternative to smaller, specialized retail outlets, but their appeal included more than the convenience of having so many products in one place. Department stores were designed to make buying pleasurable. Products were arranged elegantly, and customers were waited on courteously and promptly so that a middle-class purchaser felt that she or he had been treated as the well-to-do were treated at the smaller shops. Store managers used advertising and product displays to persuade customers to redefine their needs and desires continually. Emphasis was placed on fashionable clothing (for fashion always changes) and technologically up-to-date housewares (for technology will always provide new products). Such advertising primarily targeted women, because they managed family consumption and did most of the household spending.

Bamberger's, the most successful of New Jersey's department stores, took its message to the public by helping to establish WOR radio and by publishing *Charm* magazine. This was a stylish journal that mixed poetry, book reviews, and short stories with beautiful lithographs of the latest clothing designs, and was mailed free to the store's growing list of charge-account customers.

Bamberger's may seem a less appropriate symbol of a new economic order than, say, a textile mill might, but this is precisely what it was. The new order which it symbolized was New Jersey's consumer economy. The selling and buying of beachfront hotel rooms and the promotion of movie stars or the latest household wonder-products were just as much an industry as silk manufacturing and locomotive construction. This new economic order encompassed the birth of the automotive industry as well as the rise of professional sports. The growth of a consumer economy involved *both* the creation of new products to satisfy new wants *and* the continuous expansion of wholesaling, retailing, and advertising to assure public demand for the products. Ultimately what drove the economy was an affluent middle class with desires for leisure, play, comfort, and convenience; satisfaction of these desires was precisely what the consumer economy provided.

Persistent Poverty: The Great Depression

In the 1920s, one new game symbolized better than any other the expansion of the consumer economy: playing the stock market. To buy a stock was to win a share of industrial America, to do on a small scale what earlier had made the likes of John D. Rockefeller, Andrew Carnegie, and J. P. Morgan unbelievably rich. Specifically, purchase of a stock gave the buyer a share in the ownership of a company. For under $100 a buyer could purchase a share of stock in a company worth many millions of dollars. The buyer had two possibilities for profit. First, several times a year most companies offered stockholders' dividends, which represented a percentage of the firm's profits. Second, a buyer could profit by selling the stock for a higher price than was paid for it. In the early 1920s, agents (brokers) for individual owners traded as many as a million shares daily on the New York Stock Exchange, the most prestigious market for stocks in the world. Buying a stock with the intention of selling was, of course, risky business because prices could fall as readily as they rose.

But the 1920s were different. Prices apparently could only go up. At the end of May 1924, the average value of twenty-five industrial stocks selected by the *New York Times* was 106; at year's end, it was 134. Business was booming, profit margins were large, and stocks were a good buy. And the climb continued. When 1926 started, the industrial average stood at 181; by the end of 1927, it was 245. In December 1928, 330 was passed, and by the spring of 1929, 450 was in sight. For every dollar invested in industrial stocks early in 1924, a seller could now get back four and a half.

The game promised unending rewards, but what truly made it inviting was that it seemed almost anyone could play. The volume of transactions multiplied. Early in 1928, almost four million shares changed hands in a single day; near the end of the year, the stock exchange recorded a new high of some seven million sales; and in spring 1929, the record was pushed to over eight million shares.

And then the market crashed. It started on Wednesday, October 23, 1929. Panic followed the next day when some 9 million shares changed hands. Tuesday, October 29, set a record: 16,410,030 shares were dumped.

By November the market average was about 50 percent below the September peak of 452. Although there were periodic rallies, the trend continued downward for the next three years. In July 1932, the market reached the bottom. The average was a paltry fifty-eight. The market value of the most substantial manufacturing firms in the world was barely half of what it had been in 1924.

The stock market crash alone did not cause the Great Depression. Rather, the crash intensified a business recession (falling prices, production cutbacks, and layoffs) that had begun in the summer of 1929. Faced with potential calamity, the government, and in particular the federal Reserve System, first failed to act to stimulate the economy. It permitted interest rates to rise precipitously, making money harder to get. The crashing market, a contracting money supply, and sheer panic produced a run on the nation's banks and waves of bank failures. Prices collapsed, plants closed, and by 1933 one in every four Americans was out of work. In the large industrial cities of the Northeast and Midwest, unemployment reached fifty percent.

New Jersey suffered as badly as any other state. A look at the fate of three of the industries discussed in Chapter Two gives us some idea of the magnitude of the depression (table 8).

In measuring the human cost of the Great Depression, the employment figures (third column) most clearly indicate the extent of the tragedy. Not only did employment drop abruptly and dramatically between 1929 and 1933, but thereafter, at best, it only inched back up until the World War II economy provided new job opportunities. Many of those who lost their jobs were first- or second-generation immigrants—women in the silk industry and highly skilled workers in clay manufacturing. Here is how one Italian immigrant remembered the experience:

> I had a clock and watch business in Newark, then when the depression came in—. . . . Before I was working as a tool and die maker but then the depression came in—. . . . You know, everybody that was working, most of the people, got laid off. But I worked for a while. . . . We made all kinds of tools and dies for different companies like how they made radios. Like the RCA companies, we made lot of tools for them and things. And the company I worked for, they made tape machinery. . . . And like I say, like when the depression came in well, first half was, half of the factory was laid off and then the other; few others each week till it came down to us. I was one of the last ones since I was—I wasn't even laid off, I didn't go in. I think it got

Table 8

Industrial Decline During the Great Depression[4]

Industry	Number of Firms	Number of Wage Earners	Value Added by Manufacturing (in millions $)
Silk			
1919	686	32,326	91.6
1929	631	21,419	57.4
1933	378	10,705	16.9
1935	277*	8,242*	13.6*
1937	128*	5,875	10.2*
1939	103*	4,331*	7.8*
Clay			
1919	120	9,216	20.0
1929	120	12,137	32.4
1933	78	4,915	8.1
1935	77	5,858	11.0
1937	80	7,495	15.7
1939	76	7,268*	15.9*
Steel			
1919	16	13,811	40.1
1929	17	8,056	31.1
1933	10	4,953	8.2
1935	11	6,292	14.5
1937	12	8,915	24.3
1939	9	7,298	16.3*

NOTE: *Value added* is the increased value of a product when it is transformed from raw materials to a finished product. Data marked with stars (*) are not precisely comparable to figures for earlier years.

> down to one or two days a week. So I got a job at the WPA and there we got four dollars a day while we work three days a week. We made twelve dollars, but believe me them days with twelve dollars it's like a hundred today.... We got by because [my wife] Maria went to work. That's the only time I had Maria work. She worked in a laundry.... But after when things straighten up I didn't have Maria work. I told her to quit. She never work since, she is always a housewife.[5]

No group suffered more than New Jersey's small but growing black labor force. Having faced decades of violent racism in the South, blacks found in the labor shortages during World War I and the prosperity of the 1920s opportunities to move to the urban North. In Newark, to take one example, the black population grew from about sixty-seven hundred (or 2.7 percent of the total) in 1900 to around 38,900 (or 8.8 percent) by 1930. If jobs were menial, housing dilapidated, and racism widespread, there was the hope, common to all migrant groups, that hard work would provide a degree of economic security. The Depression destroyed that hope. It did so not simply by imposing ten years of hardship on an already impoverished work force, but also by undermining the industries that had promised unskilled nineteenth-century immigrants the possibility of limited property accumulation.

If the human costs of the Great Depression are all too clear, the long-term consequences of the economic collapse are much more difficult to evaluate. One set of consequences involved the government's relationship to the economy. After state relief efforts had proved woefully inadequate and the outgoing administration of President Herbert Hoover had moved too cautiously to address the problems of unemployment, Franklin Roosevelt assumed the presidency and offered Americans a "New Deal." Roosevelt's administration intervened in the economy in three ways: with measures such as the act establishing the Works Progress Administration in 1935, which addressed problems of unemployment; with new efforts such as the Securities Exchange Act of 1934 to regulate the economy; and with long-term efforts such as the Social Security Act of 1935 to provide greater individual security from future economic difficulties. While some of these measures provided absolutely essential relief to those who were out of work, there is little evidence that they "solved" the problems of the Great Depression or even that they constituted a coherent response to the challenge of creating a more stable and just economic system. What is clear is that the New Deal left a legacy of government supervision of the economy.

The other set of long-term consequences of the Great Depression involves the impact of the collapse on the industrial sector of the economy, and here too the story is ambiguous. The table on the silk, clay, and steel industries shows strikingly different patterns of decline. The silk industry was clearly in trouble even during the prosperity of the 1920s (between 1919 and 1929, the value added by silk production fell from 91.6 million dollars to 57.4 million). In contrast, the production of pottery and clay products grew during the 1920s, and then after hitting bottom in 1933, the industry gradually recovered. Steel works and rolling mills, like silk, suffered in the 1920s, but unlike the silk industry, they made modest improvements after 1933. For some industries, then, the Great Depression required retrenchment; for others, it speeded collapse.

The relationship of the depression to the more general reorganization of New Jersey's industrial economy can be grasped by returning to the story of Paterson's silk manufacturing companies and Trenton's iron and steel industry. Silk was already a troubled industry in the 1920s. Unrelenting competition among numerous producers and stagnating demand for the product periodically idled looms and forced layoffs of upwards of half the labor force. The long history of labor troubles, which climaxed but did not end in the great strike of 1913, won workers significant wage-and-hours concessions, but also provided mill owners incentives to move to Pennsylvania and the South where labor was cheap. Skilled weavers were forced out of factory work and compelled to open their own shops with family labor. Such small shops were even more likely than the large mills to increase production to compensate for falling prices, and consequently to force the price of silk down even more. The weavers, moreover, now had to confront suppliers, buyers, and creditors who were located outside of Paterson and who were all far more powerful financially than the proprietor of a family business.

Perhaps, though, silk would have survived if it had not been for two additional problems. One problem was competition from a new product, rayon, and such competition provided some warning of how significant technology would be to the subsequent development of New Jersey industry. Silk manufacturers denounced rayon as a "cheap imitation," but by the mid-1920s, the synthetic substitute had won wide public acceptance. The second problem was fatal: the outbreak of World War II cut off American manufacturers from Japan, one of their chief sources of supply of raw silk.

Silk was already a sick industry when the Great Depression overwhelmed Paterson. The Depression destroyed almost half the city's firms. In more prosperous times, many producers might have switched to rayon, but rayon manufacturing never really took hold in Paterson. Left behind were small shops run chiefly by skilled immigrants who had scraped together enough capital to set up a couple of looms. Employing family laborers who could be paid less than regular wage earners, these shops competed for commission work but seldom captured enough business to stay in operation more than a few years. Paterson was no longer Silk City, and for its immigrant weavers it had become a place of fading dreams.

In contrast, the Great Depression marked only a temporary setback for Trenton's iron and steel industries. By 1939 employment in iron and steel had climbed to a higher level than before the crash of 1929, and it continued to grow, so that by 1947, there were some eighteen thousand people in Trenton employed in the metal industries and the manufacture of machinery. John A. Roebling's Sons Company operated four plants, three in Trenton and one in nearby Roebling, covering some 217 acres; in 1951, it had an annual payroll of 23 million dollars and employed some five thousand workers. Its products included cable, covered and uncovered wire, aviation cable, telephone wire, and steel nets; its finer wire products were used in typewriters, textile machines, umbrellas, and countless other products.

The early 1950s marked the high point of industrial employment in Trenton. From that time to the present, employment in the metal industries has gradually declined. The Roebling concerns were sold in 1952 to the Colorado Fuel and Iron Corporation; in 1962, one of the company's four main plants stopped producing wire and was sold, with a loss of some 250 jobs; in 1968, the company announced plans to consolidate its

Trenton operations into a single plant, and transferred its business offices to Roebling; and in 1969, the company was sold to another corporation that closed down the remaining wire works. In Trenton as a whole, there were still some 10,000 workers employed during the 1970s in the metal and machine industries, but these companies represented a reduced share of a declining manufacturing sector.

The different fates of the silk and iron industries suggest that even now it is too early to evaluate fully the impact of the Great Depression. Historical significance is a question of *effect over time,* and many of the consequences of the Depression on employment, industrial structure, and urban life are still working themselves out. Whether the poverty of the urban poor and the decay of industrial cities that the Great Depression so brutally reinforced are permanent features of New Jersey society simply cannot yet be answered.

The Post-Depression Economy

In the short run, then, New Jersey's industrial economy was badly battered, and it was only revived by the vigorous recovery brought about by World War II. In the long run, in contrast, two trends persisted across the twentieth century: the sustained growth of the labor force despite the curtailment of European immigration; and the rapid expansion of the service sector of the economy.

While the increase in the size of the labor force can be explained primarily in terms of natural (reproductive) population growth, there have been two other significant sources of additional labor. Over the past few decades a growing number of women have sought paid employment, and people have left agricultural work in the South for industrial and service employment in the North. In 1920, one-fifth of all workers were women; today more than two-fifths of the labor force is female. Female employment has moved out of manufacturing and domestic service into the retail trades, business services, and professions. Whereas in 1920 only three females in twenty were employed for pay, now more than seven in twenty are. The other notable source of new workers has been migration from the South. Between 1910 and 1960, an estimated nine million southerners (of whom about half were white and half were black) left the region. Some left during World Wars I and II when northern employment opportunities improved; some left because they were black and racial discrimination in the North was not as bad as in the South; some left because the boll weevil destroyed their cotton crop or because their landlords forced them off the land they farmed; and many left because their relatives had already gone North and offered to help them find jobs and places to stay (table 9). No one story can possibly

Table 9

Women and Blacks in the Work Force[6]

Year	Number of Women Employed	% of All Employed	Number of Blacks Employed	% of All Employed
1900	154,500	20.4	36,200	4.8
1920	296,000	22.6	61,700	4.7
1940	448,900	28.6	73,200	4.7
1960	762,800	32.5	194,400	8.3
1980	1,402,100	42.6	343,500	10.4

convey a complete sense of why and how southerners came North, but these excerpts from a 1980 interview with a black woman who moved from South Carolina to New Jersey provide some idea of what migrants left behind.

> I was born in Clinton, South Carolina. . . . I left Clinton, I think it was in 1926, and I went to work on James Island [South Carolina] as a parish worker. And I worked there for five years until I was married. Then I came to Plainfield. James Island is off the coast of Charleston. It's just across the Ashley River and it's—I think it's about nine by nine square miles. When I worked on James Island the population was about 90 percent black and about 10 percent white. Most of the white people that were on the island were farmers and they ran truck farms. And black people worked for them. They raised beans, tomatoes, melons, and . . . white potatoes. These were some of the main crops they had. Most of the black people raised cotton and some raised beans and anything that they could get a little money right away or, you know, a market.[7]

An excerpt from an interview with another southern black female migrant, who left Georgia and came to New Jersey about

1940, describes the type of work that awaited many women and blacks when they initially entered the paid labor force:

> I planned to get a job and to work. And at that time work was very hard to find. So, what I did, I took a sleep-in job. And I slept-in for two years. And then I returned back to my mother. And I stayed there two weeks and then I came back to New Jersey. And I went back to my job and went to work again. I didn't have any skills. Only learning how to clean a house. And then after I came to New Jersey I worked in domestic work for two and a half years. Then I worked in a factory, the Crispy Kernel Nut Factory, for about seven or eight months. And then along came the war and I got a job in the factory as a welder. And I stayed there for about seven years.[8]

The women and blacks who joined New Jersey's modern work force shared with the European immigrants of the nineteenth century the common desire to make a better living; the opportunities the twentieth-century economy held out to them, however, were different. Table 10 indicates how rapidly the structure of New Jersey's economy has changed since World War II. The table illustrates three changes which appear to be of lasting significance, and which will together provide a conclusion to our survey. Agriculture has declined and continues

Table 10

Percentage of Labor Force in Each Sector of the New Jersey Economy, 1950–1983[9]

	1950	1983
Agriculture	3.8	.6
Government	9.9	16.9
Manufacturing	48.9	26.3
Service	37.4	56.2

to shrink in terms of importance in twentieth-century New Jersey. Manufacturing has declined as well, although not nearly as much. In their place, the consumer economy, or the service sector, has expanded rapidly.

The demise of the Garden State's farm economy is striking. At the turn of the century, New Jersey had over thirty-four thousand farms; in 1920, the number had fallen to twenty-nine thousand; by 1980, fewer than ten thousand remained. In the nineteenth century, grain farming had been lost to the Midwest, where the soil was cheaper and richer and the land flatter, but feeding the growing urban-immigrant population gave New Jersey farmers the healthy alternatives of dairying and vegetable growing. These markets still exist, but in large measure they are no longer served by local farmers. Why not?

The story is chiefly one of technology. Ironically, the technological advances that have helped American agriculture have undercut New Jersey farming. Most critically, the harvesting of vegetables has been largely mechanized. As with wheat farming in the nineteenth century, the mechanization of agriculture proved most profitable when farmers could use their machines on extensive tracts of flat, inexpensive land—and that New Jersey did not have. As shippers introduced new refrigeration techniques and better roads and trucks made long hauling possible, New Jersey's farmers sold their lands to housing developers and industrial builders.

Farming has not disappeared, of course, and especially in the Delaware River counties much of the land is still used for vegetable and fruit growing and for dairying. In 1981, New Jersey ranked in the top four states in the production of blueberries, cranberries, asparagus, tomatoes, spinach, and several other crops, and its dairy and livestock industry generated some $125 million in receipts. By way of comparison, however, manufacturing produced over $30 billion worth of goods.

Manufacturing, the mainstay of the nineteenth-century economy, has also declined in relative importance, but in absolute terms it has grown considerably. Between 1919 and 1980, value added increased from $1.4 billion to $30.1 billion. The Great Depression battered New Jersey's traditional growth industries (textiles, silk, iron, pottery), yet otherwise left the manufacturing sector intact. This resulted, as table 11 indicates, in a reordering of New Jersey's industrial structure. The ranking is based on employment figures.

The textile industry, to take one example, has suffered considerably, and the decline that earlier in the century affected the silk industry has now spread to the clothing industry generally. Between 1972 and 1982, employment in textiles dropped from 69,700 workers to 50,800, a much sharper drop than occurred nationwide. Employment in chemical manufacturing, on the other hand, has remained relatively stable, and with

Hand harvesting and mechanized harvesting of field crops. *The mechanized harvesting of vegetables has been one factor in the shift of vegetable farming from the East to the West and Southwest, where land is flatter and less expensive. Courtesy* MARK SINGLEY, RUTGERS UNIVERSITY.

Table 11

Industries in New Jersey by Number of Workers, Twentieth Century[10]

Rank	1919	1983
1	Shipbuilding	Chemicals
2	Silk	Electrical & electronic products
3	Electrical machinery	Textiles & apparel
4	Machine shop products	Nonelectrical machinery
5	Textile dyeing	Printing & publishing
6	Steel	Fabricated metals
7	Worsted goods	Food processing
8	Chemicals	Rubber & plastics
9	Rubber	Instruments
10	Phonographs	Paper

53,700 workers in 1982, the industry surpassed all others in the state. Among the most important employers are E. I. DuPont de Nemours, based primarily in Salem County, and specializing in bulk chemicals; BASF Wyandotte, a Parsippany corporation which employs some four thousand workers to make products ranging from agricultural chemicals to vitamins and antifreeze; and Exxon, with plants in Linden and Bayonne and research laboratories in Florham Park and Clinton. In general, New Jersey's problem is no different from that afflicting all the Northeast. Rebuilding factories to handle new products or improved production processes, and retraining workers generally costs more in New Jersey and the Northeast than it costs to establish new industries in other, less heavily developed areas of the United States where living costs are lower, transportation and other support services newer, and land for construction less expensive.

A shift toward high-technology industries might revive the manufacturing economy, but to date such a shift has not occurred. During the 1970s, perhaps one manufacturing job in six was in a high-technology industry. About a quarter of the state's industrial output came from such firms. High-tech industries produce such products as electronic computing equipment, semiconductors, engineering and scientific instruments, and surgical and medical equipment, and are engaged in such processes as book publishing, the preparation of industrial inorganic chemical, and making adhesives and sealants. But while computer products have flooded the consumer market, there has been little growth in the industries that make such products in New Jersey, and that growth has been no better than in other states.

Among the more vigorous of the new industries (see the 1983 list) is printing. In the post-depression economy, printing was not a major industry, and was restricted primarily to newspaper publishing. Between 1972 and 1982, employment in the New Jersey printing and publishing industry grew from about forty-two thousand to almost fifty-four thousand workers, making it the fifth largest manufacturing enterprise in the state. During this period, the industry generated between two and three billion dollars annually in revenues, and ranked sixth in the nation.

One fundamental change in this industry has been the replacement of hot metal composition (which was done by linotype machines) with computer-directed, technologically advanced photoreproduction processes. Web presses can print multiple colors simultaneously on both sides of paper that is fed through at speeds of up to fifty thousand copies per hour, and relay the output to machines that fold, glue, and bind it just as rapidly. The final product may be anything from a book to an insert that will go to millions of people nationwide. Computers are used at every stage of the process, from preparing negatives to balancing colors, controlling ink flow, and handling financial records. Such technological innovations in traditional industries may well be the best measure of how New Jersey's manufacturing economy will do in the future.

In the short run, however, the most notable feature of the modern economy (as well as theme of this chapter) has been the persistent growth of consumer-oriented businesses and services. In 1983, as we have seen in the table on employment in 1950 and 1983, the service and government sectors of the economy (those most directly tied to consumption) accounted for more than two-thirds of the state's employment. If textiles and iron led the nineteenth-century economy, small businesses (food stores, automotive dealers, restaurants), wholesalers, and state and local government have created most of the new jobs of recent years.

Technological development has also directly affected the service sector of the economy. In 1982, about 14 percent of the employment in service industries (corresponding to 3 percent of all nonagricultural employment) was in high-technology concerns. Between 1977 and 1982, employment in computer programming, data processing, and computer-related services jumped by two thirds, from 11,667 to 19,447. Even more dramatic has been the continued growth of the communications industry, from 41,414 service employees in 1977 to 57,691 in 1982, a growth rate nearly twice the national average. While technologically oriented industries are only one part of the service economy, their growth clearly has stimulated the continuing expansion of other opportunities in the state's economy.

Thus by the late twentieth century, the nature of New Jersey's economy has been fundamentally altered. People no longer work merely for food and shelter, but for sports cars and condominiums. The question remains whether the consumer economy can continue to keep New Jersey prosperous. And if New Jersey prospers, will the gap between rich and poor grow wider, or will everyone be better off?

Epilogue

More than half a century after the tragedy of Katherine Schaub and the radium dial painters, their virtually forgotten story still has meaning for New Jersey. Despite the shift from basic production industries toward consumption and service concerns, economic growth still carries with it enormous, often hidden costs for workers, consumers, and others. These costs became tragically apparent again in the 1980s.

In January 1984, the appellate division of the New Jersey Superior court upheld a jury award of punitive damages to James Fisher in his suit against the Johns-Manville Corporation. Fisher had worked for a Passaic County asbestos company supplied by Johns-Manville from 1938 to 1942. As the court explained: "His duties required him to handle asbestos in various forms, causing him regularly to inhale dust. He never wore any protective clothing or apparatus and was never given any cautionary warning or instruction in the safe handling of asbestos either by his employer or by the suppliers."[11]

Asbestos is a mineral and a fibrous structure that can be spun or felted to make noncombustible fabrics for heat and insulation; in the twentieth century, it has been used widely in wallboards, shingles, and tiles in most homes and public buildings, including schools. The production process, at least until recently, created large quantities of dust (finely pulverized asbestos) that workers would inhale and bring home on their clothes and skin. In Manville, it was once common practice to refer to the clouds of asbestos dust as "snow in July" and to joke about the way it turned laborers into snowmen (in a way reminiscent of the jokes made by radium workers who glowed in the dark).

Except for a brief period in 1945, Fisher did not again work with asbestos, but in 1977, doctors determined that he was badly ill and that asbestos was the cause. Treatment led to the side effects of diabetes and arthritis, and in 1979 he was hospitalized with bronchitis. His lung condition compounded by his smoking, Fisher was unable to return to work, but he brought suit against the suppliers of asbestos both for failure to warn him of the dangers and for deliberately withholding information they had available about the risks of working with asbestos. The suppliers responded that in the 1930s they had not known of the dangers. The jury agreed with Fisher and the appellate court upheld their verdict.

H. W. Johns and Charles Manville were both fairly typical nineteenth-century entrepreneurs. Johns invented a new roofing material in 1858 by running together asbestos, burlap, jute, and pitch. In 1886 Manville, a failed gold prospector, opened a business insulating furnaces with cement. After Johns died in 1898 of "dust phthisis pneumonitis" (probably asbestosis), Manville bought out the concern and formed Johns Manville in Brooklyn. In 1912, the company moved from Brooklyn to a 328-acre plot in Somerset County, New Jersey; by 1929, the working community that had grown up around the company had about five thousand residents, many of them eastern and southern European immigrants, and the borough of Manville was incorporated. A fully integrated company that mined asbestos and processed and marketed roofing and insulation products, Johns-Manville survived the Great Depression and became one of the most successful corporations in the United States in the post–World War II era. A prosperous manufacturing company, it was also a part of the consumer economy, supplying products for home construction and automobile production.

As early as the first decade of the century, there were medical warnings that asbestos might be dangerous. In 1918, the United States Bureau of Labor Statistics published a report noting a high death rate among asbestos workers, and throughout the 1930s, asbestos workers with health problems filed claims under workman's compensation laws. While juries have accepted evidence that asbestos manufacturers, according to evidence juries have accepted, knew of these medical dangers from a very early date and did little about them, public information about the health hazards of asbestos emerged slowly. Part of the problem is that there is a long latent period between exposure to asbestos and the time when asbestosis and other diseases manifest themselves—asbestos is a "time bomb" in the body waiting to go off. The first health studies to receive wide dissemination appeared in the 1960s; these studies reported an alarmingly high rate of asbestosis (which becomes debilitating) among workers who had been exposed at least twenty years before and much higher death rates for asbestos workers than in the general population from lung and gastrointestinal cancers.

A great many lawsuits followed against Johns-Manville and other asbestos manufacturers; by August 1982, when Johns-Manville took advantage of the federal bankruptcy laws to bring the suits to a temporary halt, there were, by one count, some 165,000 cases pending. The bankruptcy proceedings did not destroy Johns-Manville; rather, the company was reorganized and part of its future earnings were set aside to pay compensation claims. The company had already begun to diversify into other products; in 1973 it had moved its corporate headquarters to Denver; and in 1985 it closed the doors on its complex in Manville. Left behind were the problems of homes and schools insulated with asbestos and of workers, like James Fisher, incurably afflicted with an industrial disease.

CONCLUSION

This book began by asking a set of related questions: How rapidly did New Jersey's economy grow and who benefited from this growth? How readily did New Jersey's economic structure change in response to market conditions? That is, how readily were new occupations and industries added and unprofitable ones abandoned? What were the costs of economic progress? Reviewing the conclusions of each chapter will suggest some answers.

In the seventeenth and eighteenth centuries, European settlers systematically expanded a *farming economy* across the colony. The accomplishment of this economy was to allow an ever-growing number of people to live as comfortably as earlier generations had done. The benefits were greatest for those who held the most land and entrepreneurial capital; they were least for Afro-American slaves and the Lenape Indians.

The Lenape either died from diseases brought from Europe or were forced off their lands. With them perished a *subsistence economy* made possible by abundant resources, limited wants, and little or no population growth. Europeans cleared the land, introduced domesticated animals, and planted for profit. In doing so, they transformed New Jersey's forests, making the land more productive but destroying much of the animal and plant life they found there.

In the nineteenth century, an *industrial economy* and an urban culture sprang from a still-agricultural state. The accomplishment of the industrial economy was to let an even larger and continuously growing population slowly improve its standard of living. Some, of course, benefited far more than others. The wealth of industrialists stood in sharp contrast to the tenement poverty of immigrant workers, and it was small comfort to those who were tired, cold, and hungry to know that eventually things might improve somewhat. Still, most immigrants had left worse conditions in Europe and had come expecting to work hard, and if they survived industrial accidents, there was a promise of some security for them and their families.

In the late nineteenth and early twentieth centuries, New Jersey's economy was again transformed. A producer society became a *consumer society.* Of course, all manufactured goods are produced to be consumed. What made this period different was the growing affluence of middle- and working-class Americans and the rapid multiplication of desires that this affluence allowed. People demanded more and had the money to afford it. Goods unknown in the early nineteenth century became necessities in the middle-class household of the twentieth century, and time spent before in the factory could now occasionally be spent on the leisurely pursuit of pleasure.

To say this is to argue that New Jersey's economy has been one of *abundance:* an abundance of agricultural products, an abundance of industrial goods, an abundance of consumer items. But the uses of that abundance have left two unresolved problems.

One is waste. A people of plenty have become a people of waste. In the hunger for profit, the price of economic improvement has not always been considered. The price has been, in both human and environmental terms, a waste of individual and natural resources. To be sure, some dangers were not apparent to the people who made the tradeoff between profit and harm; but too often, the goal of progress has been an excuse for ignoring the human and environmental price of that progress. In human terms, the most notable cost has been the health (and occasionally the lives) of industrial workers, as the slow and unexpected death of Katherine Schaub and the asbestos workers should remind us. In environmental terms, the cost is measured in what the drive to clear fields, dam rivers, build mills and factories, and crisscross the state with roads, canals, and railways has done to the animal population, the watersheds and drinking water, the air, and the natural beauty of the landscape.

Nor has abundance solved the problem of poverty. The poor have always been a part of New Jersey society. What has changed has been the awareness of poverty and the explanation for the situation. Since the Great Depression, it has been difficult to ignore the fact of poverty or to blame the poor for their own plight. Rather, the Great Depression serves as a stark reminder that economic conditions over which the individual has no control can overtake even the most prosperous people in the world and force them into a decade of want and desperation. What makes the current problem particularly difficult is the connection between race and poverty. In 1979, while approximately one white family in twenty lived below the poverty level (defined as less than $3,000 in family income), one in four black and Hispanic families earned that little or less. In 1986, the poverty rate among blacks in the northeast states remained about 25 percent, while in comparison, only about 9 percent of the white population lived in poverty.

The nineteenth-century response was a growing industrial economy that promised unskilled immigrants some degree of security. It is unclear whether the consumer economy of the twentieth century can provide either enough jobs for the unskilled or the skills needed for meaningful employment. The future of society clearly rests on how states like New Jersey and nations like the United States deal with the problems of poverty and waste.

NOTES

Full citations are found in "Sources," p. 100.

Introduction

1. Burlington County Probate Records, no. 7945.

Chapter One

1. "Letter of Isaack de Rasieres," 107.
2. Ibid.
3. "From the 'Korte Historiael,'" in *Narratives of Early Pennsylvania,* 220.
4. "Letter of Isaack de Rasieres," 107.
5. "Present State of the Colony," 192–94.
6. Thomas, "An Historical and Geographical Account of Pennsylvania," 345–57.
7. Erkuries Beatty Farm Diary.
8. Elizabeth Crane Diary.
9. Burlington County Probate Records, no. 8389.
10. *Archives of the State of New Jersey,* 26: 89.
11. *Archives of the State of New Jersey,* 28: 48.
12. Boyer, *Early Forges & Furnaces,* 18–19.

Chapter Two

1. *Merritt v. Parker,* 1 Coxe (2nd ed.) 527 (1795).
2. Gordon, *Gazetteer of the State,* 207.
3. *Rogers Locomotive Catalog,* 15.
4. *Occupations at the Twelfth Census,* 666–69; *Twelfth Census, Population,* pt. 1, 463.
5. Benson, *Peter Kalm's Travels in North America,* 117.
6. Gordon, *Gazetteer of the State,* 251.
7. Schuyler, *The Roeblings,* 121.
8. "The Brooklyn Bridge," 946.
9. Turk, "Trenton, New Jersey in the Nineteenth Century," 207–09.

10. *Fourteenth Census, State Compendium,* 44–45.
11. Bureau of Statistics, *Annual Report* (1883), 131.
12. Bureau of Statistics, *Annual Report* (1903), 261–62.
13. Bureau of Statistics, *Annual Report* (1904), 109–11, 188–95.
14. Gordon, *Gazetteer of the State,* 106.
15. Sipes, *Pennsylvania Railroad,* 183–84.
16. John Ten Ecyk Diary.

Chapter Three

1. Clark, "Glowing in the Dark," has informed my discussion of this issue.
2. *Fourteenth Census, State Compendium: New Jersey,* 52–57.
3. Eastman, *Zanesville,* 61–73. The study focused on midwestern communities of twenty thousand to thirty-five thousand people; such communities were wealthier and had smaller working-class populations than New Jersey's industrial cities.
4. *Fifteenth Census, Manufactures,* II, 338, 842–43, 951; *Biennial Census of Manufactures, 1933,* 176, 407–8, 459; *Biennial Census of Manufactures, 1935,* 383–84, 826–27, 925; *Biennial Census of Manufactures, 1937,* 402–08, 847, 977; *Sixteenth Census, 1940: Manufactures,* II, pt. 1, 68, 90–118, 308–313; III, 626.
5. Edited version of L. T. interview, by Josephine Halmo, New Jersey Multi-Ethnic Oral History Project, New Jersey Historical Commission, Trenton. The name in the text has been changed.
6. *Occupations at the Twelfth Census,* 336–42; *Fourteenth Census, State Compendium,* 2, 52, 56; *Sixteenth Census, Population,* III, pt. 4, 165–68, 181, 185; *Eighteenth Decennial Census, Population,* I, pt. 32, 171, 172; *1980 Census of Population,* I, chap. C, pt. 32, 102–3, 120.
7. Edited version of R. T. Interview, by Myrna Wasserman, New Jersey Multi-Ethnic Oral History Project, New Jersey Historical Commission, Trenton.
8. Edited version of M. S. Interview, by Delores Sheppard, New Jersey Multi-Ethnic Oral History Project, New Jersey Historical Commission, Trenton.
9. New Jersey Economic Policy Council . . . , *New Jersey Profile,* 39.
10. *Fourteenth Census, State Compendium,* 52–57; *New Jersey Profile,* 97–98.
11. *Fisher v. Johns-Manville Corp.* 193 N.J. Super. 113 (1984), 116.

SOURCES

Introduction

Burlington County Probate Records, no. 7945, New Jersey State Archives, Trenton

Chapter One

Archives of the State of New Jersey, ed. William A. Whitehead, et al., 1st and 2nd ser., 42 vols. (Newark, 1880–1949), vols. 26, 28

Erkuries Beatty Farm Diary, 1797–1800, MS. 897, The New York Historical Society, New York

Charles S. Boyer, *Early Forges & Furnaces in New Jersey* (Philadelphia, 1931), 17–23

Burlington County Probate Records, no. 8389, New Jersey State Archives, Trenton

Elizabeth Crane Diary, Special Collections, Alexander Libraries, Rutgers University, New Brunswick

Dorothy Cross, *New Jersey's Indians,* New Jersey State Museum Report no. 1, (Trenton, 1965)

"From the 'Korte Historiael Ende Journaels Aentycheninge' by David Pietersz de Vries, 1630–33, 1644," in Narratives of Early Pennsylvania, West New Jersey and Delaware, 1630–1707, ed. Albert C. Myers (New York, 1912), 7–29

"From the 'Korte Historiael Ende Journaels Aentycheninge' by David Pietersz de Vries, 1633–43," in *Narratives of New Netherland, 1609–1664,* ed. Franklin Jameson (New York, 1909), 186–234

"Letter of Isaack de Rasieres to Samuel Blommaert, 1628," in *Narratives of New Netherland,* 102–15

James H. Levitt, *For Want of Trade: Shipping and the New Jersey Ports, 1680–1783* (Newark, 1981)

"The Present State of the Colony of West-Jersey, 1681," in *Narratives of Early Pennsylvania,* 191–95

Gabriel Thomas, "An Historical and Geographical Account of Pennsylvania and of West-New-Jersey," in *Narratives of Early Pennsylvania,* 313–52

Peter O. Wacker, *Land & People. A Cultural Geography of Preindustrial New Jersey: Origins and Settlement Patterns* (New Brunswick, 1975)

Chapter Two

Adolph B. Benson, *Peter Kalm's Travels in North America* (New York, 1937)

"The Brooklyn Bridge," *Harper's New Monthly Magazine* 67 (December 1882–May 1883), 925–46

Thomas C. Corkran, ed., *The New American State Papers: Manufactures*, 9 vols. (Wilmington, Del., 1972), 6:158–60

H. Jerome Cranmer, *The New Jersey Canals: State Policy and Private Enterprise, 1820–1832* (New York, 1978)

Stuart Galishoff, *Newark: The Nation's Unhealthiest City, 1832–1895* (New Brunswick, 1988)

Thomas F. Gordon, *Gazetteer of the State of New Jersey* (Trenton, 1834)

Herbert G. Gutman, "The Reality of the Rags-to-Riches 'Myth': The Case of the Paterson, New Jersey, Locomotive, Iron, and Machinery Manufacturers, 1830–1880," in Gutman, *Work, Culture & Society in Industrializing America* (New York, 1976), 211–33

Howard Harris, "The Transformation of Ideology in the Early Industrial Revolution: Paterson, New Jersey: 1820–1840" (Ph.D. diss., City University of New York, 1985)

John A. Herbst and Catherine Keene, *Life and Times in Silk City: A Photographic Essay of Paterson, New Jersey* (Haledon, N.J., 1984)

Reese V. Jenkins and Paul B. Israel, "Thomas Edison: Flamboyant Inventor," *IEEE Spectrum* 21 (December 1984): 74–79

Reese V. Jenkins et al., eds., *The Making of an Inventor, February 1847–1873*, vol. 1 of *The Papers of Thomas A. Edison* (Baltimore, 1989)

Poor's Manual of the Railroads of the United States, 1904 (New York, 1905)

Mary Alice Quigley and David E. Collier, *A Capital Place: The Story of Trenton* (Woodland Hills, Calif., 1984)

George L. A. Reilly, "The Camden and Amboy Railroad in New Jersey Politics, 1830–1871" (Ph.D. diss., Columbia University, 1951)

The Rogers Locomotive Catalog, 1876, intro. John H. White (Newark, 1983)

Hamilton Schuyler, *The Roeblings: A Century of Engineers, Bridge-builders, and Industrialists* (Princeton, 1931)

William B. Sipes, *The Pennsylvania Railroad: Its Origins, Construction, Condition, and Connections* (Philadelphia, 1875)

John Ten Eyck Diary, 1855–1859, Special Collections, Alexander Library, Rutgers University, New Brunswick

Jesse Rose Turk, "Trenton, New Jersey in the Nineteenth Century: The Significance of Location in the Historical Geography of a City" (Ed.D., Columbia University, 1964)

Rudolph Vecoli, *The People of New Jersey* (Princeton, 1965)

Richard F. Veit, *The Old Canals of New Jersey, A Historical Geography* (Little Falls, N.J., 1963)

GOVERNMENT PUBLICATIONS

Annual Statements of the Railroad and Canal Companies of the State of New Jersey . . . from the Year 1904, in *Documents of the One Hundred and Twenty-Ninth Legislature of the State of New Jersey,* 4 vols. (Trenton, 1905), vol. 1

Digest of Accounts of Manufacturing Establishments in the United States and of Their Manufactures (Washington, D.C., 1823)

New Jersey Bureau of Statistics of Labor and Industry, *Annual Reports* (Trenton, 1883, 1903, 1904, 1912)

Social Aspects of Child Labor in New Jersey, 1903: Monograph on Economic Topics Collected from the Annual Reports of the Bureau of Statistics of New Jersey (Trenton, n.d.)

BUREAU OF THE CENSUS PUBLICATIONS
(order is chronological)

Population of the United States in 1860 (Washington, D.C., 1864)

Report on the Social Statistics of Cities: pt. 1, The New England and Middle States (Washington, D.C., 1886)

Twelfth Census of the United States Taken in the Year 1900: Population, pt. 1 (Washington, D.C. 1901)

Occupations at the Twelfth Census (Washington, D.C. 1904)

Thirteenth Census of the United States, 1910, Abstract . . . Supplement for New Jersey (Trenton, 1913)

Fourteenth Census of the United States, State Compendium, New Jersey (Washington, D.C. 1925)

LEGAL CASES

Merritt v. Parker, 1 Coxe (2nd ed.) 527 (1795)

Society for Establishment of Useful Manufactures et al. v. The Morris Canal and Banking Company, 1 Saxon (Court of Chancery Reports) 157 (1830)

Chapter Three

W. Elliot Brownlee, *Dynamics of Ascent: A History of the American Economy* (New York, 1974)

Paul Brodeur, *Outrageous Misconduct: The Asbestos Industry on Trial* (New York, 1985)

Claudia Clark, "Glowing in the Dark: the Radium Dialpainters, the Consumers' League, and Industrial Health Reform in the United States, 1910–35" (Ph.D. diss., Rutgers University, 1991)

Jeff Coplon, "Left in the Dust," *The Village Voice* 28, no. 9 (1 March 1983)

Ruth Schwartz Cowan, *More Work for Mother: The Ironies of Household Technology from the Open Hearth to the Microwave* (New York, 1983)

John T. Cumbler, *A Social History of Economic Decline: Business, Politics, and Work in Trenton* (New Brunswick, 1989)

R. O. Eastman, Inc., *Zanesville and 36 Other American Communities: A Study of Markets and of the Telephone as a Market Index* (New York, 1927)

Audrey Olsen Faulkner, et al., eds., *When I Was Comin' Up: An Oral History of Aged Blacks* (Hamden, Conn., 1982)

Salmon J. Flink, et al., *The Economy of New Jersey* (New Brunswick, 1958)

Charles E. Funnell, *By the Beautiful Sea: The Rise and High Times of That Great American Resort, Atlantic City* (reprint; New Brunswick, 1983)

John Kenneth Galbraith, *The Great Crash, 1929* (Boston, 1954)

Steve Golin, *The Fragile Bridge: The Paterson Silk Strike, 1913* (Philadelphia, 1988)

Jack Temple Kirby, *Rural Worlds Lost: The American South, 1920–1960* (Baton Rouge, La., 1987)

Philip J. McLewin, "Labor Conflict and Technological Change: The Family Shop in Paterson," in *Silk City: Studies on the Paterson Silk Industry, 1860–1940,* ed. Philip B. Scranton (Newark, 1985), 135–58

New Jersey Multi-Ethnic Oral History Project, New Jersey Historical Commission

Richard A. Noble, "Paterson's Response to the Great Depression," *New Jersey History* 96 (Autumn/Winter 1978): 87–98

John E. O'Connor and Charles F. Cummings, "Bamberger's Department Store, Charm Magazine, and the Culture of Consumption in New Jersey, 1924–1932," *New Jersey History* 102 (Fall/Winter 1984): 1–33

"Occupational Death," *Maclean's* 93 (19 May 1980)

"Petrochemicals: Our no. 1 Industry," *New Jersey Business* 30 (August 1984): 30–34

Clement A. Price, "The Afro-American Community of Newark, 1917–1947: A Social History" (Ph.D. diss., Rutgers University, 1975)

James T. Prior, "Our Printing Industry Is Undergoing Graphic Change," *New Jersey Business* 32 (June 1984): 40–50

Stanton G. Richards, "Trenton's Roebling and Sons Wire-Rope Plant: Its Rise, Fall, Sale, and Closure," unpublished paper, 1985

John A. Roebling's Sons Company, *Roebling Handbook* (Trenton, 1947)

Katherine Schaub, "Radium," *Survey Graphic* 68 (May 1932): 138–41

Philip B. Scranton, Introduction to *Silk City,* 1–8

Paul C. Spehr, *The Movies Begin: Making Movies in New Jersey, 1887–1920* (Newark, 1977)

Marie Stoeckel, *An Evaluation of Asbestos School Survey Programs in*

New Jersey, Connecticut, and Rhode Island (New Haven, Conn., 1978)

Trenton Times, 5 March 1951, 9 December 1952, 16 December 1968

Robert Paul Vogel, "The Broad Silk Industry in Paterson, New Jersey: A Troubled Industry in Microcosm 1920 Through 1935" (Ph.D. diss., New York University, 1980)

GOVERNMENT PUBLICATIONS

Brainpower; High Technology in New Jersey (n.p., 1983)

New Jersey Department of Health, "Asbestos Policy Committee's Report to the Governor" (Trenton, 1985)

New Jersey Economic Policy Council and Office of Economic Policy, *Fifteenth Annual Report* (Trenton, 1983), *Seventeenth Annual Report* (Trenton, 1985), and *New Jersey Profile* (Trenton, 1984)

Report of the Governor's Commission on Science and Technology for the State of New Jersey (Trenton, 1983)

James E. Wood, *Employment Experience of Paterson Broad-Silk Workers, 1926–1936,* Works Progress Administration, National Research Report, no. 1–3 (Philadelphia, Pa., 1939)

BUREAU OF THE CENSUS PUBLICATIONS
(order is chronological)

Twelfth Census of the United States Taken in the Year 1900, Population, pt. 1 (1901)

Occupations at the Twelfth Census (1904)

Fourteenth Census of the United States, State Compendium: New Jersey (1925)

Fifteenth Census of the United States, Manufactures, 1929. II, *Report by Industries,* and III, *Report by States* (Washington, D.C., 1933)

Biennial Census of Manufactures, 1933 (Washington, D.C., 1936); 1935 (Washington, D.C., 1938); 1937 (Washington, D.C., 1939)

Sixteenth Census of the United States, 1940: Manufactures, 1939. II, *Report by Industries,* and III, *Reports for States and Outlying Areas* (Washington, D.C., 1942)

Sixteenth Census of the United States: 1940, Population. III, *The Labor Force,* pt. 4, *Nebraska–Oregon* (Washington, D.C., 1943)

Census of Manufactures: 1947. III, *Statistics by States* (Washington, D.C., 1950)

Census of Manufactures: 1958. III, *Area Statistics* (Washington, D.C., 1961)

Eighteenth Decennial Census of the United States, Census of Population, 1960. I, *Characteristics of the Population,* pt. 32: *New Jersey* (Washington, D.C., 1961)

1967 Census of Manufactures. III, *Area Statistics* (Washington, D.C., 1971)

1980 Census of Population. I, *Characteristics of the Population,* chap. C, *General Social and Economic Characteristics,* pt. 32, *New Jersey* (Washington, D.C., 1983)

1982 Census of Manufactures, Geographic Area Series, New Jersey (Washington, D.C., 1985) and *Poverty in the United States, 1986* (Washington, D.C., 1988)

LEGAL CASE

Fisher v. Johns-Manville Corp., 193 N.J. Super. 113 (1984)

SUGGESTIONS FOR FURTHER READING

Surprisingly few works have been written specifically on New Jersey's economy. In the absence of such studies, there are several ways to reconstruct the state's economic history. I began with trips to some of the region's historic sites. Barbara Hudgins, *Trips and Treks: A Guide to Outings in New Jersey and Beyond* (Green Village, N.J., 1983) is all that is needed to start. Among the most interesting sites are Longstreet Farm in Holmdel Park, where seasonal agricultural activities are carried out as they were in the 1890s; the American Labor Museum in the Botto House in Haledon, where films and exhibits depict Paterson's silk era; and the Mercer Museum in Doylestown, Pennsylvania, which contains a superb collection of agricultural and artisanal tools. Both The New Jersey Historical Society (230 Broadway, Newark 07104) and the New Jersey Historical Commission (4 North Broad St., CN 305, Trenton 08625-0305) regularly publicize historical exhibitions and events.

Primary sources (documents from the period being studied) are particularly valuable; many are published and available in libraries. For the colonial period, begin with the *New Jersey Archives* series; included in its volumes are reprints of Pennsylvania and New York newspaper stories about East and West Jersey (until the 1770s, there were no newspapers in New Jersey) that give rich detail on farming conditions in the region. Two books of narratives, J. Franklin Jameson, ed., *Narratives of New Netherland, 1609–1664* (New York, 1909) and Albert Cook Myers, ed., *Narratives of Early Pennsylvania, West New Jersey, and Delaware, 1630–1707* (New York, 1912), recount how some of the first European settlers saw the lands along the Hudson and Delaware Rivers.

For the nineteenth century, the most valuable primary sources are city histories. These were generally written by residents and chronicled the efforts of local entrepreneurs to establish specific industries. See, for example, L. R. Trumbell, *A History of Industrial Paterson—Silk, Cotton, Flax, Locomotive, Iron, and Miscellaneous Industries* (Paterson, 1882). Such local histories can be put in context by using United States census reports; these are listed in Henry Dubester, *Catalog of United States Census Publications, 1790–1945* (New York, 1968). Even more valuable are state publications, which through 1904 are indexed in Adelaide Rosalie Hasse, *Index of Economic Material in Documents of the States of the United States, New Jersey, 1789–1904* (Washington, D.C., 1914, 1965). I relied particularly on the annual reports of the New Jersey Bureau of Statistics of Labor and Industry, and, for the more recent period, on the reports of the Economic Policy Council, headed by Joseph J. Seneca of Rutgers, The State University.

Economic history cannot be separated from agricultural history or from the history of work and labor, nor should one think about how an economy developed without thinking about the society of which that economy was a part. For this reason, many of the most useful secondary sources deal with economic history as only one aspect of a many-faceted story. Several books are unusually valuable in this regard. Peter O. Wacker's *Land & People. A Cultural Geography of Preindustrial New Jersey: Origins and Settlement Patterns* (New Brunswick, 1975) is especially good on the Lenape Indians and population growth. The institutional and political context in which early economic development took place is covered in Richard P. McCormick's *New Jersey from Colony to State, 1609–1789* (Princeton, 1964).

The Lenape Indians are the subject of Dorothy Cross, *New Jersey's Indians* (Trenton, 1965), and more recently of Herbert C. Kraft, *The Lenape: Archaeology, History, and Ethnology* (Newark, 1986). More generally, see Bruce Trigger, ed., *Handbook of North American Indians,* vol. 15: *Northeast* (Washington, D.C., 1978).

For urban New Jersey, two short, fully illustrated essays were useful: John A. Herbst and Catherine Keene, *Life and Times in Silk City: A Photographic Essay of Paterson, New Jersey* (Haledon, N.J., 1984), and Mary Alice Quigley and David E. Collier, *A Capital Place: The Story of Trenton* (Woodland Hills, Calif., 1984); as well as John Cumbler, *A Social History of Economic Decline: Business, Politics and Work in Trenton* (New Brunswick, 1989). The canal era is covered by Richard F. Veit,

The Old Canals of New Jersey, A Historical Geography (Little Falls, 1963), while the best popular biography of Thomas A. Edison is Matthew Josephson, *Edison: A Biography* (New York, 1959). The early history of Atlantic City is told beautifully in Charles E. Funnell, *By the Beautiful Sea: The Rise and High Times of That Great American Resort: Atlantic City* (New York, 1975, New Brunswick, 1983).

As good a place as any to find a general history of the American economy is W. Elliot Brownlee, *Dynamics of Ascent: A History of the American Economy* (New York, 1974). For the history of New Jersey, the many works of John T. Cunningham are valuable, but see specifically his *Made in New Jersey: The Industrial Story of a State* (New Brunswick, 1954). The themes of the conclusion can be pursued in David M. Potter, *People of Plenty: Economic Abundance and the American Character* (Chicago, 1954), and Lester C. Thurow, *The Zero-Sum Society: Distribution and the Possibilities for Economic Change* (New York, 1980).